Evelyn De Morgan: 101 Masterpieces

By Maria Tsaneva

First Edition

*****

Evelyn De Morgan: 101 Masterpieces

Foreword

Evelyn De Morgan (1855 – 1919) was an English Pre-Raphaelite painter. During her lifetime Evelyn De Morgan produced approximately 102 oil paintings and over 300 drawings. At first glance, works like Flora (1894), Cadmus and Harmonia (1877), Eos (1895) and Night and Sleep (1878) appear to be that of a typical mid-century literary painter influenced by the work of Spencer Stanhope, Watts and Burne-Jones. Consequently, this was the way in which most contemporary critics assessed her paintings: Many do reflect the usual conventions and literary themes of late Victorian art with its Pre-Raphaelite traces and neo-classical tendencies. However, looking closer, one discovers Symbolist works that employ the language of Christian allegory to reveal the artist's engagement with the contemporary issues of her time. These works may be divided into three categories: spiritualist allegories, depictions of sacred heroines, and war paintings.

She was born Evelyn Pickering to upper middle class parents. Evelyn was educated at home and started drawing lessons when she was 15. On the morning of her seventeenth birthday, Evelyn recorded in her diary, "Art is eternal, but life is short...I will make up for it now, I have not a moment to lose."

She went on to persuade her parents to let her go to art school. At first they discouraged it, but in 1873 she was enrolled at the Slade School of Art.

Her uncle, John Roddam Spencer Stanhope, was a great influence on her works. Evelyn often visited him in Florence where he lived. This also enabled her to study the great artists of the Renaissance; she was particularly fond of the works of Botticelli. This influenced her to move away from the classical subjects favoured by the Slade school and to make her own style.

In 1887, she married the ceramicist William De Morgan. They lived together in London until he died in 1917. She died two years later on 2 May 1919 in London and was buried in Brookwood Cemetery, near Woking, Surrey.

George Frederic Watts said of Evelyn De Morgan: "I look upon her as the first woman artist of the day — if not of all time".

There is a permanent exhibition of some of her best-known works at the De Morgan Centre in Wandsworth, London.

Paintings and Drawings

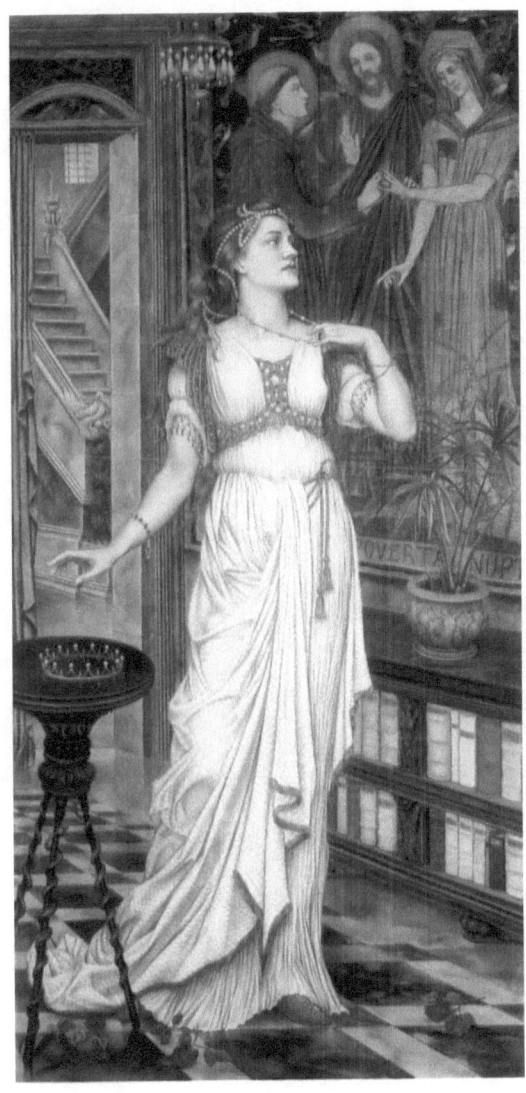

The Crown of Glory, 1896
Oil on canvas

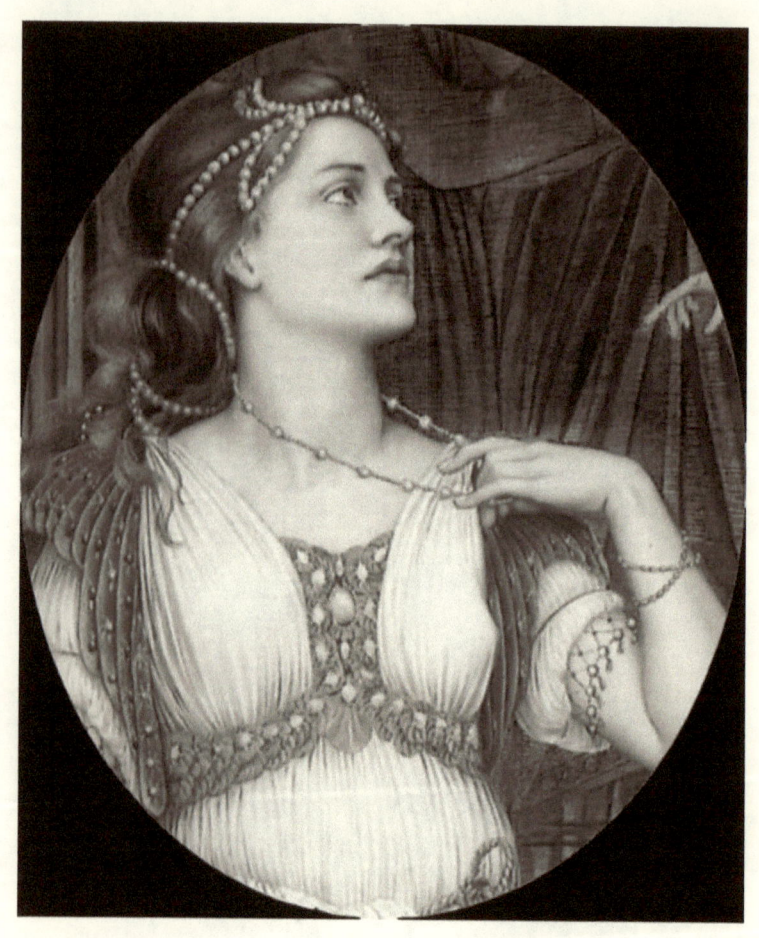

Detail

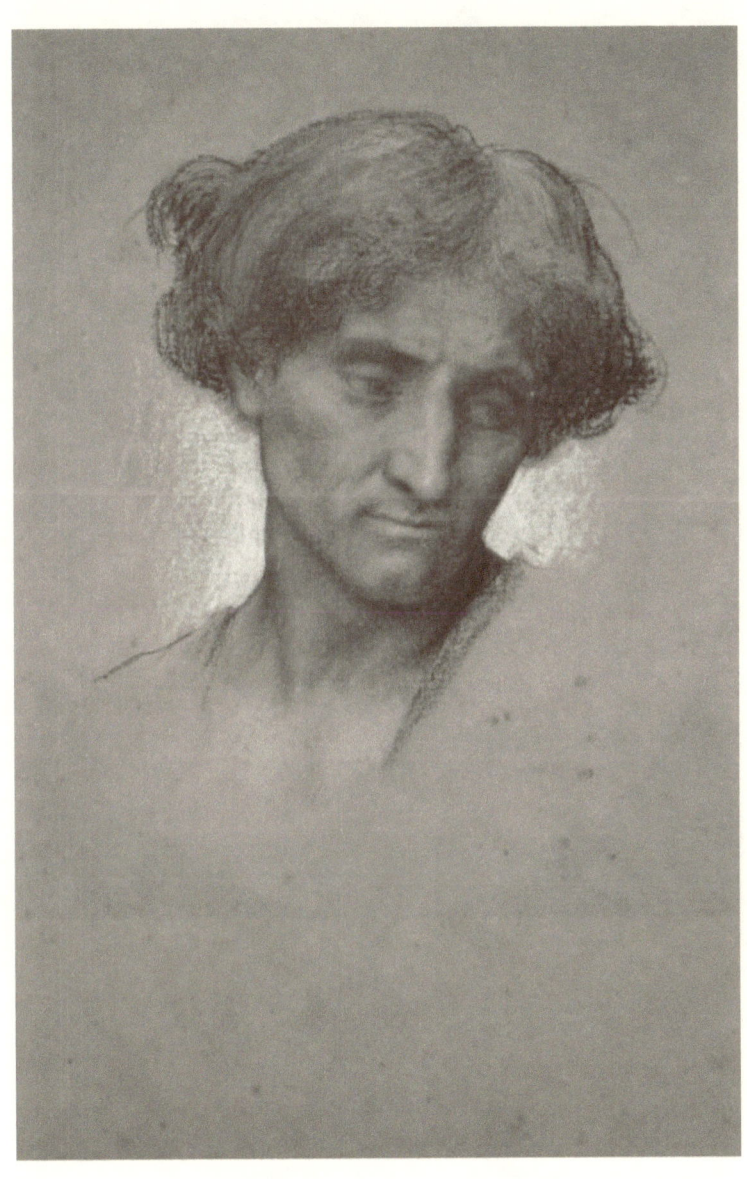

Study of a male head, 1914

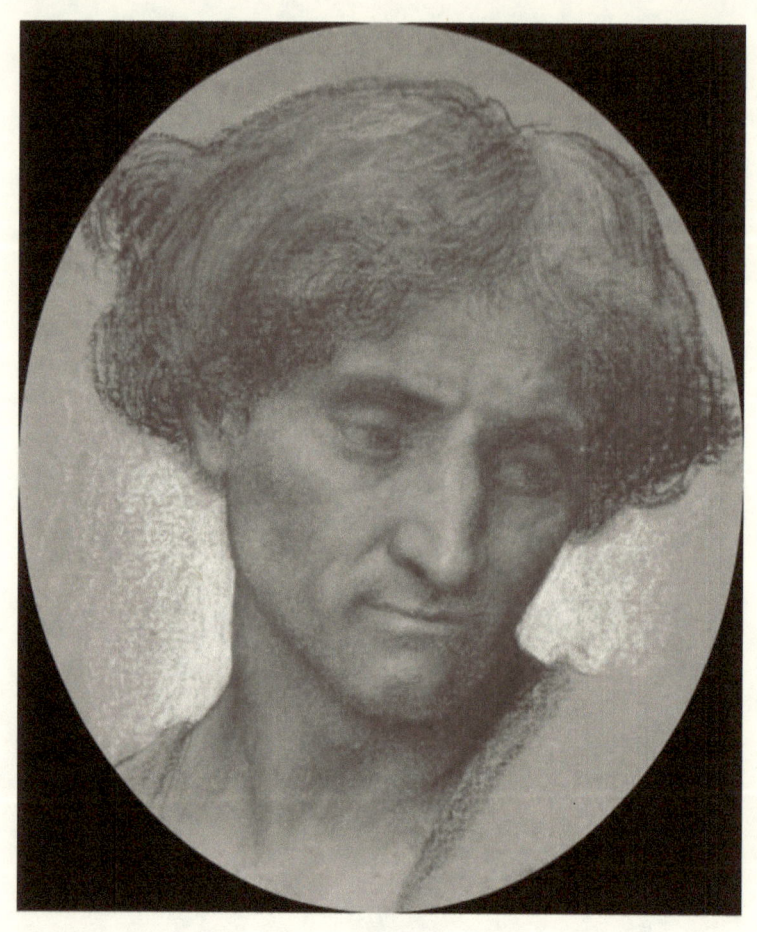

Detail

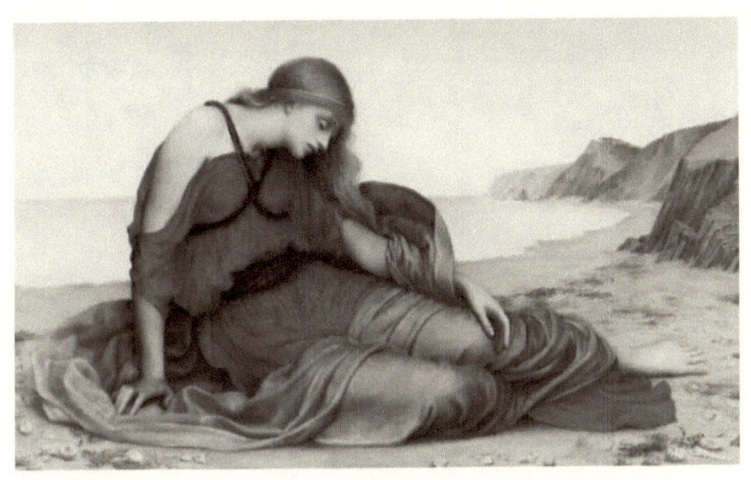

Ariadne in Naxos
Oil on canvas

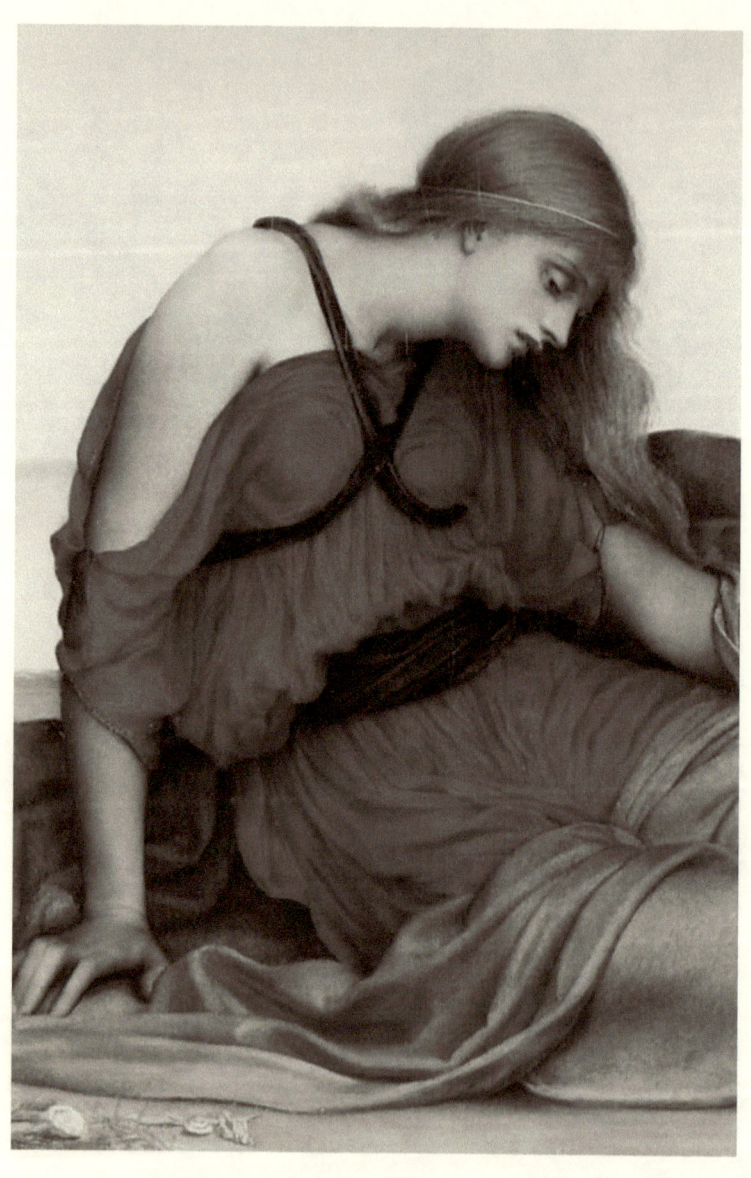

Detail

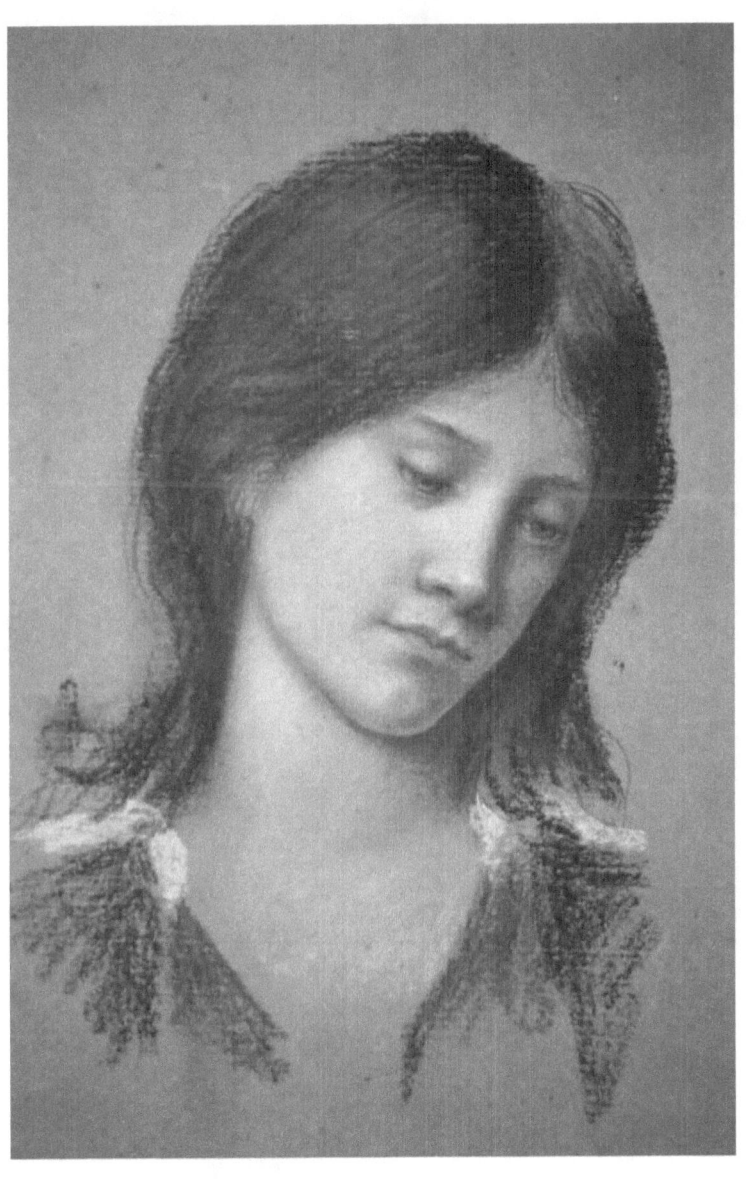

Study of female head for 'Our Lady of Peace'
Pastel on brown paper

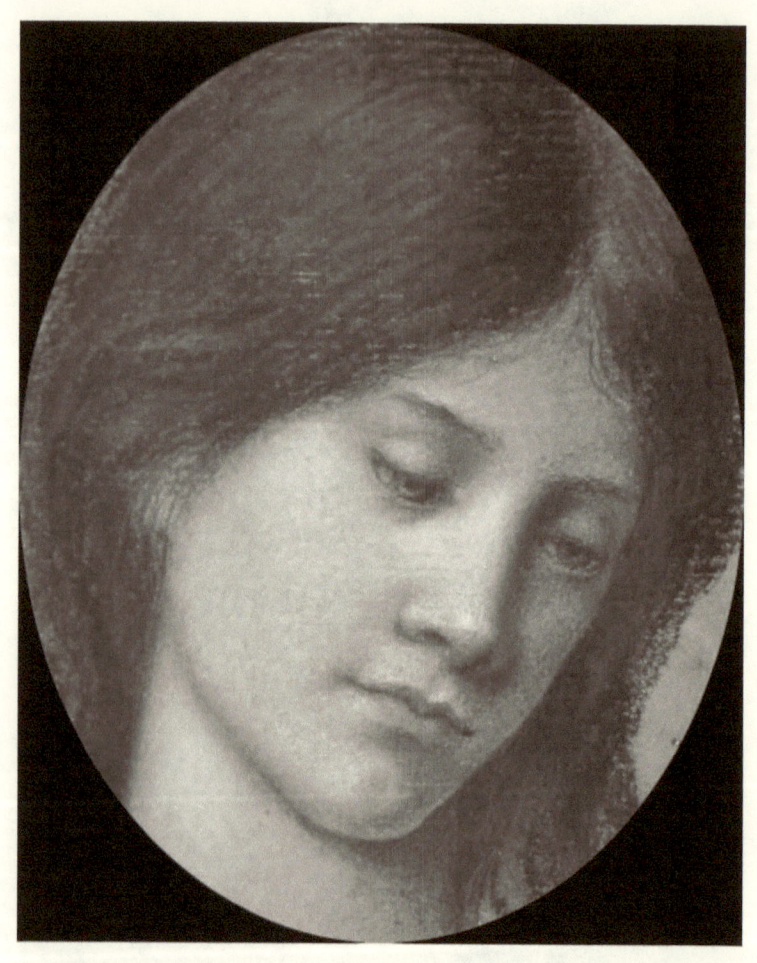

Detail

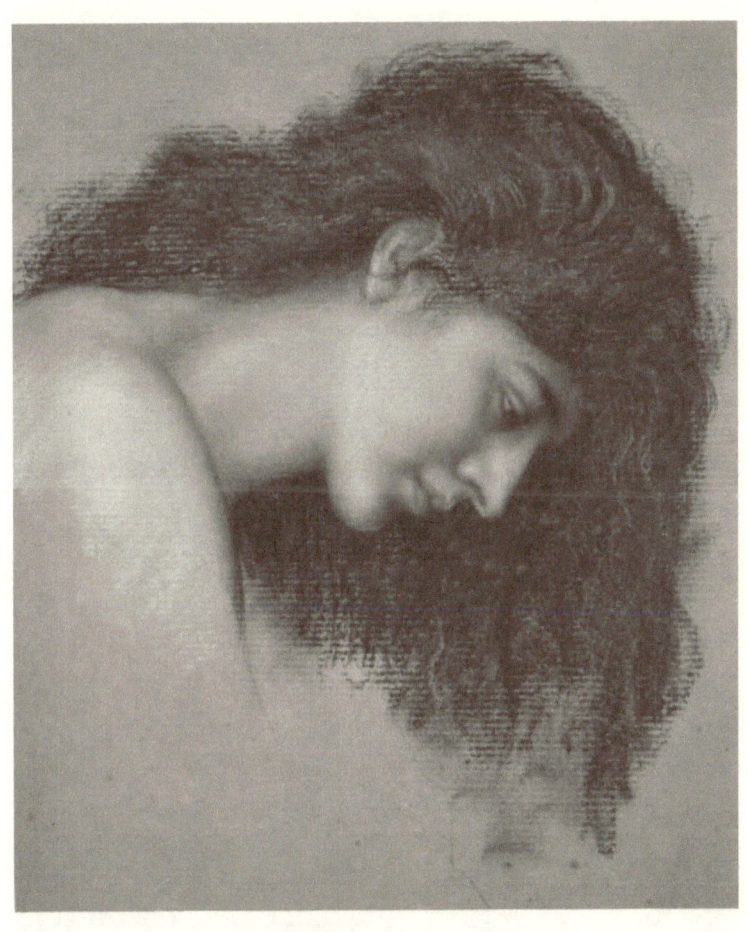

Study of a female head for 'The Cadence of Autumn', 1905

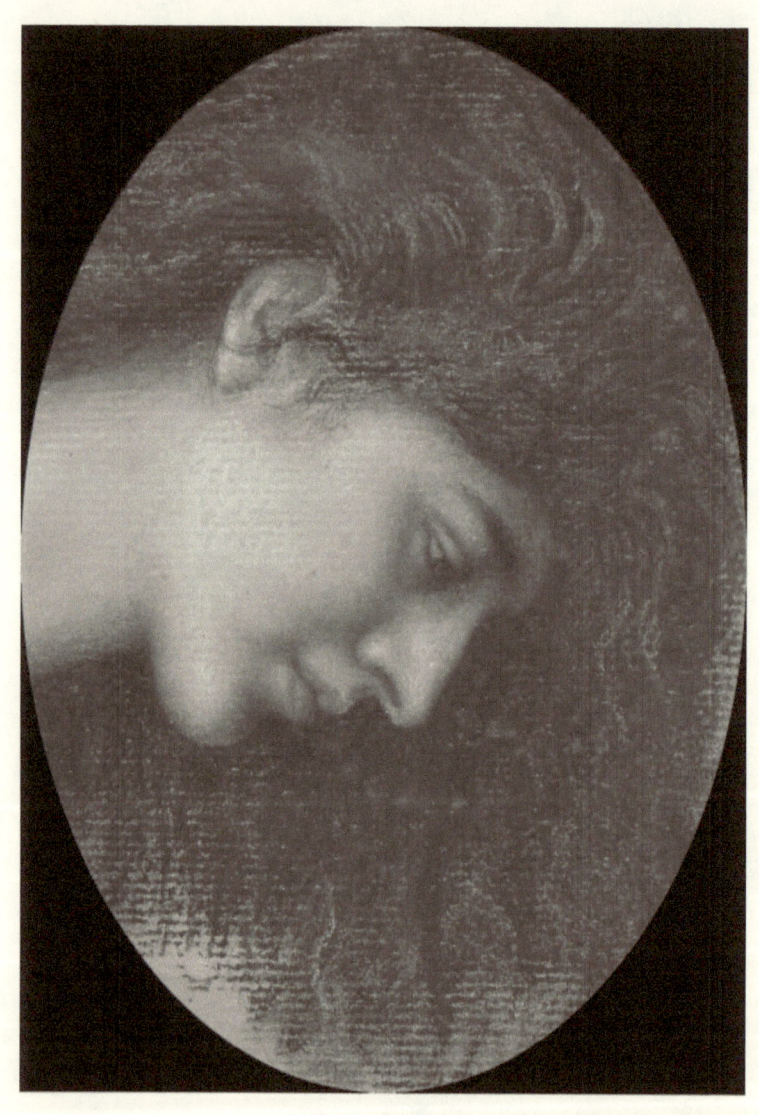

Detail

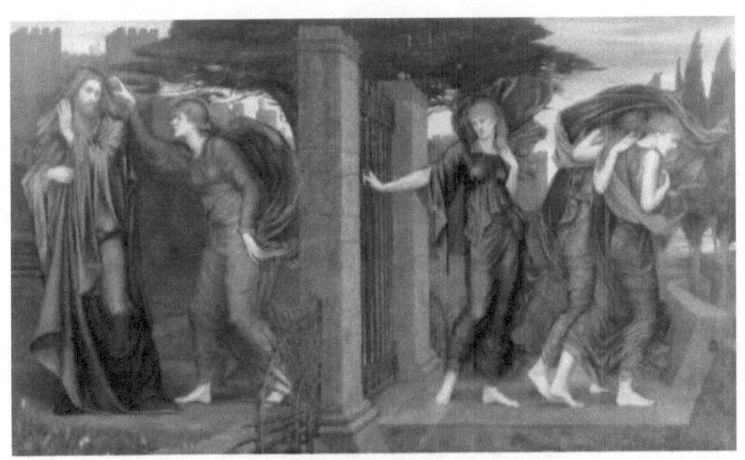

The Grey Sisters
Oil on canvas

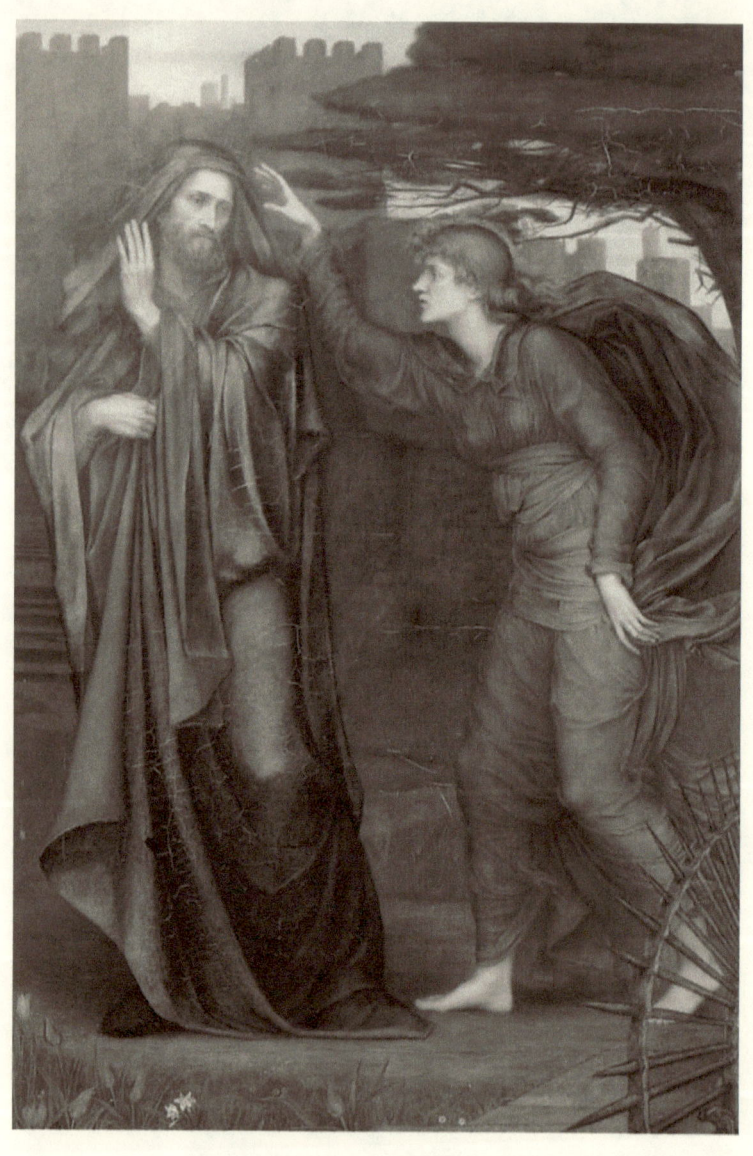

Detail

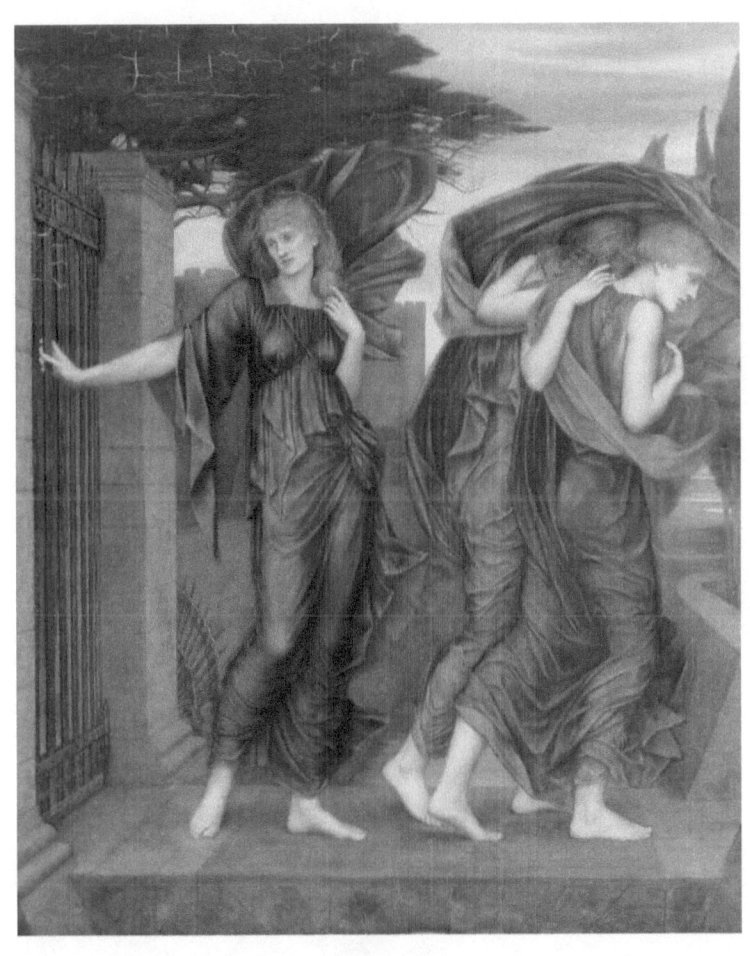

Detail

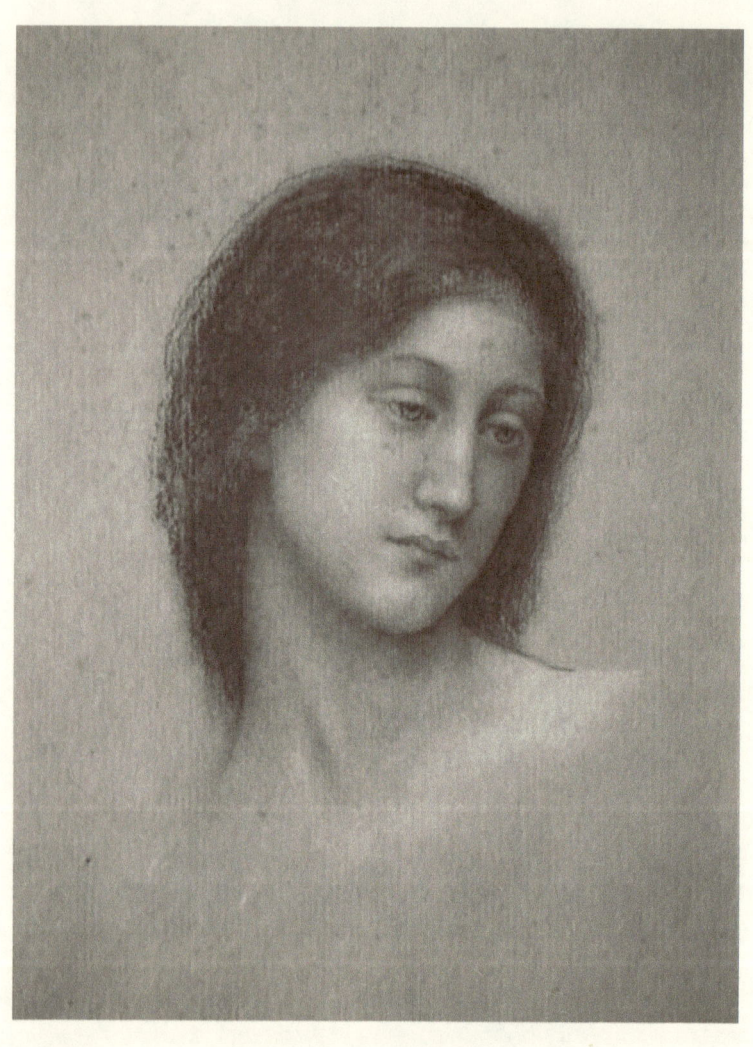

Study of a female head for 'The Red Cross', 1916

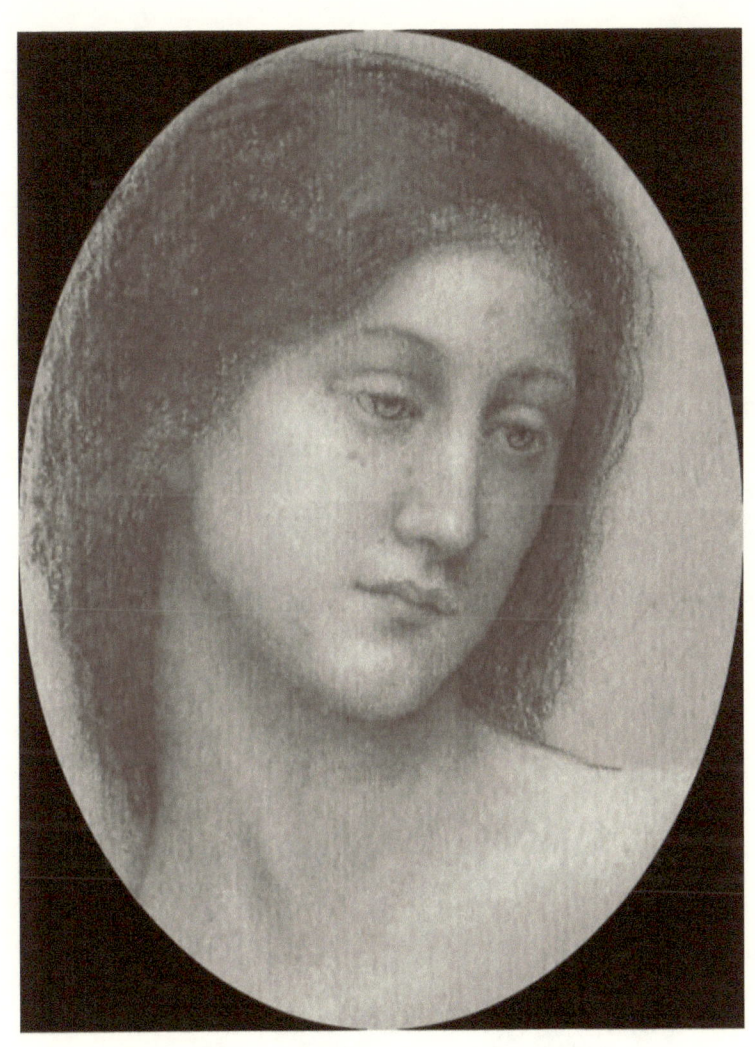

Detail

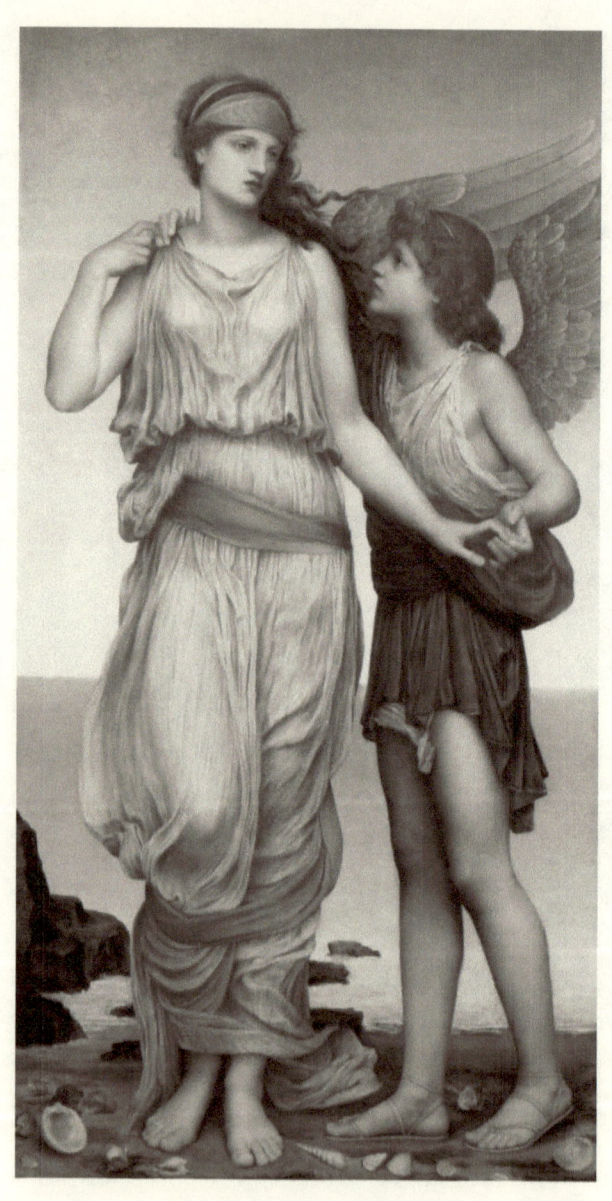

Venus and Cupid, 1878
Oil on canvas

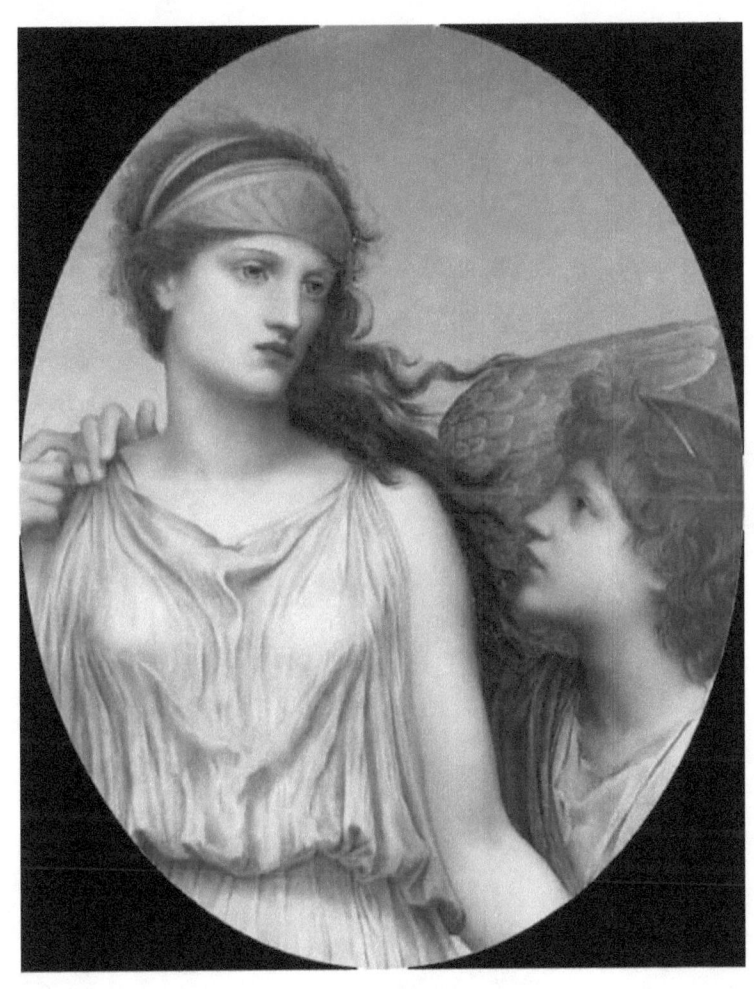

Detail

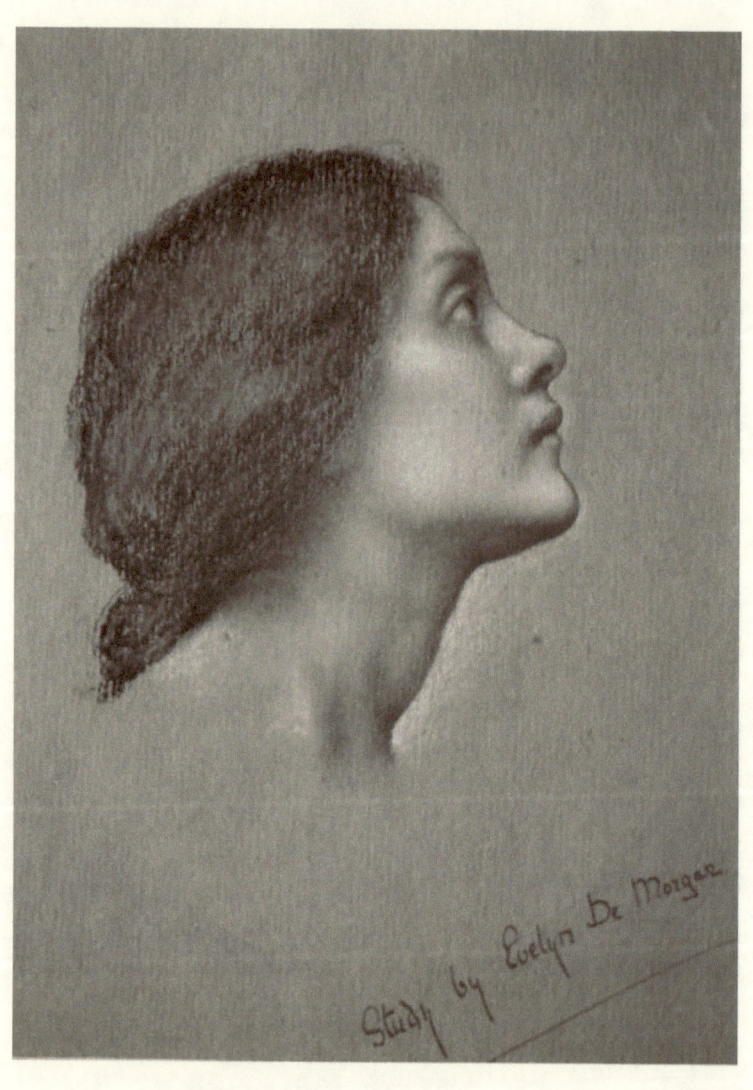

Study of a female head in profile
Pastel on brown paper

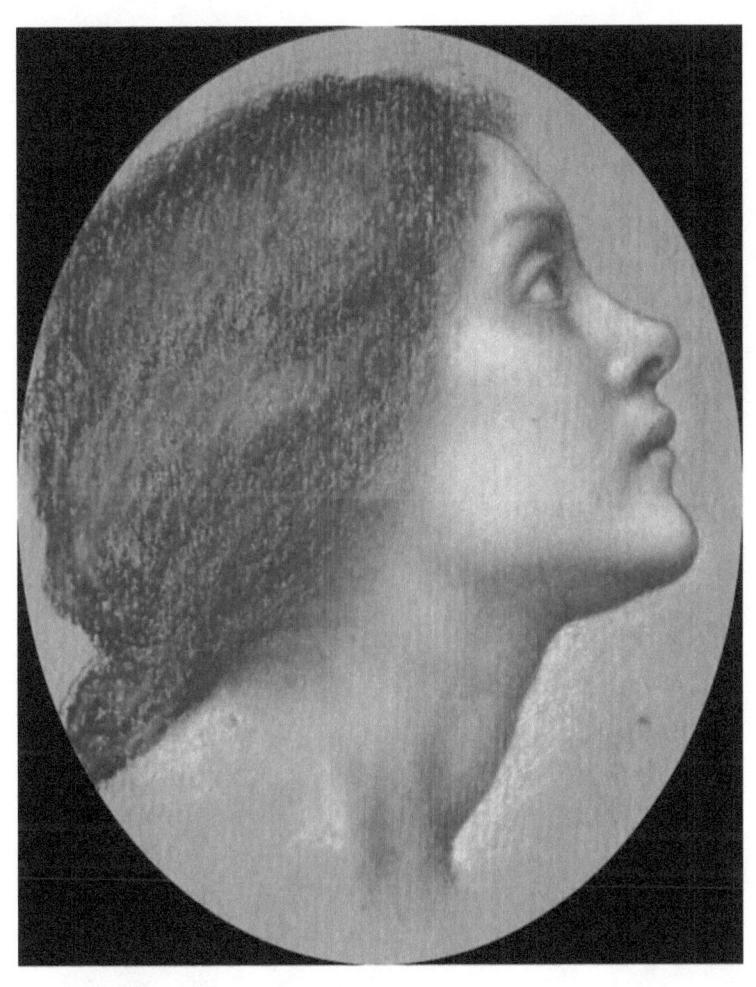

Detail

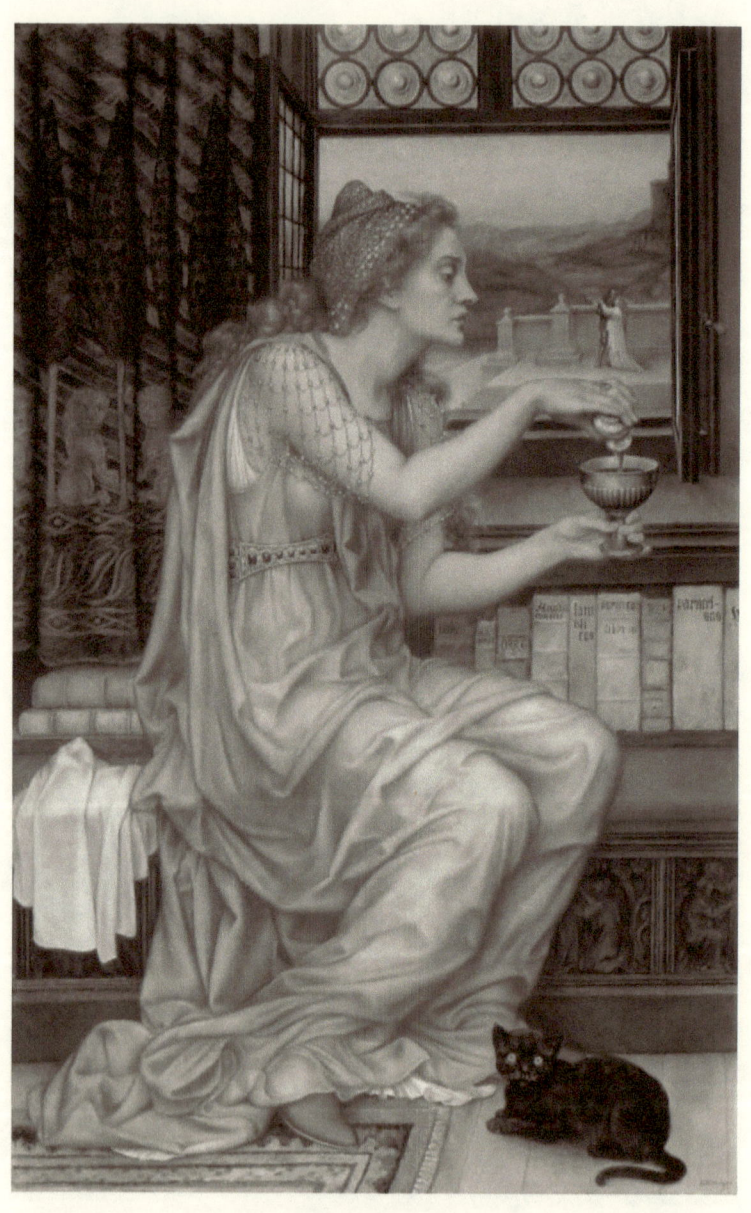

The Love Potion, 1903

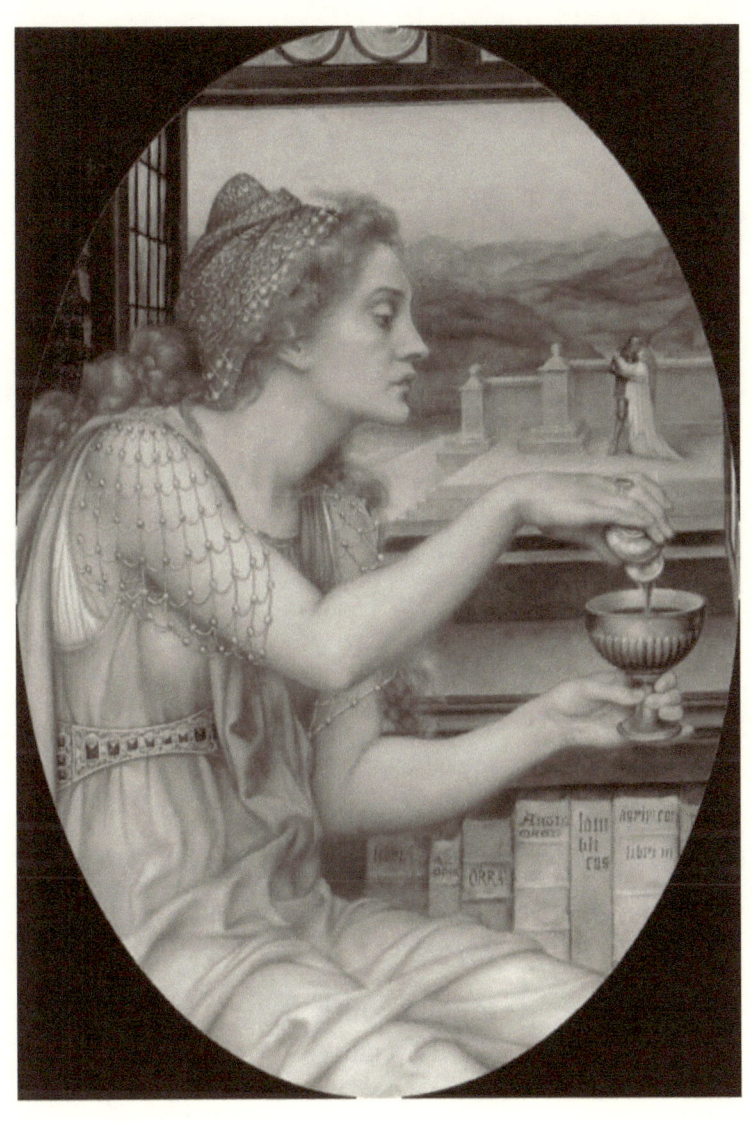

Detail

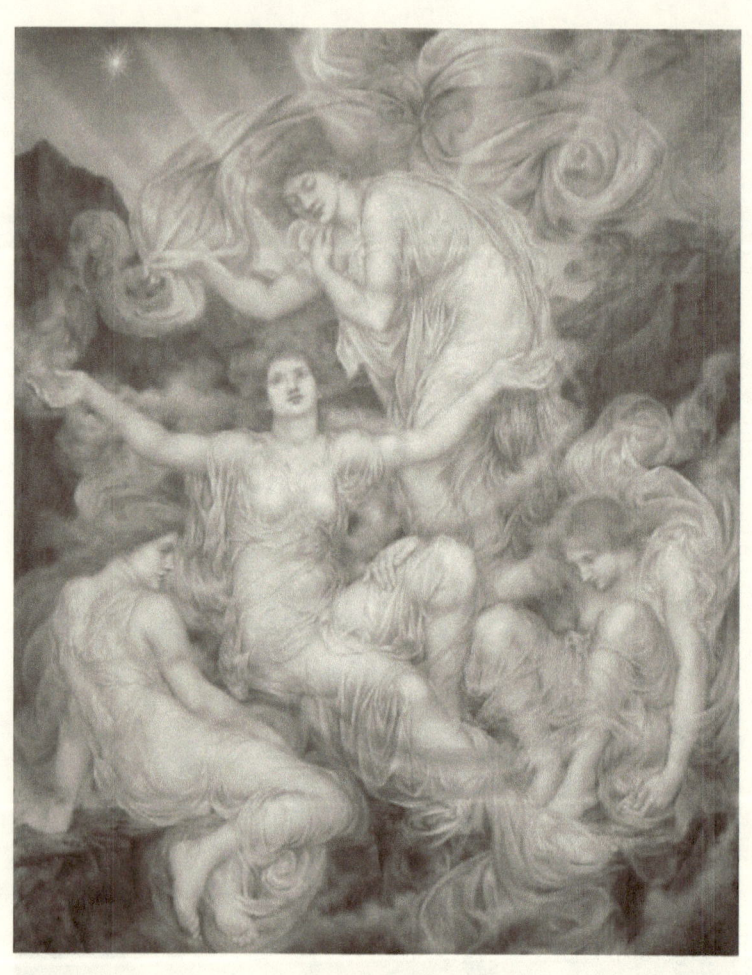

Daughters of the Mist
Oil on canvas

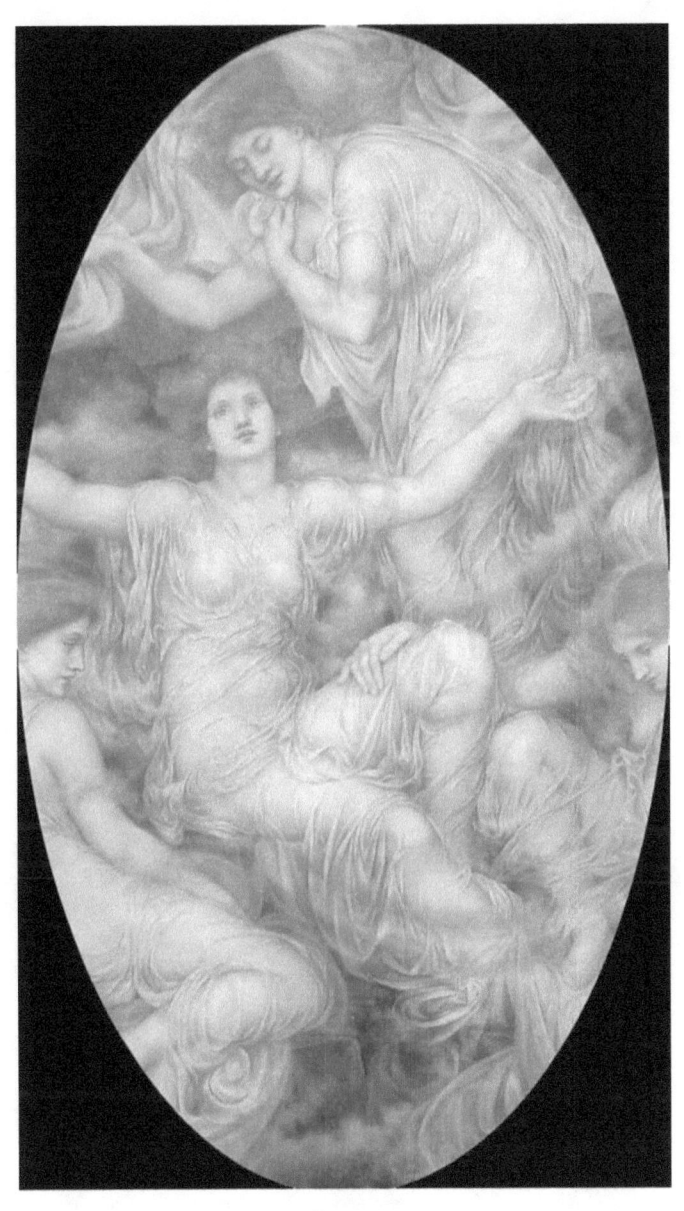

Detail

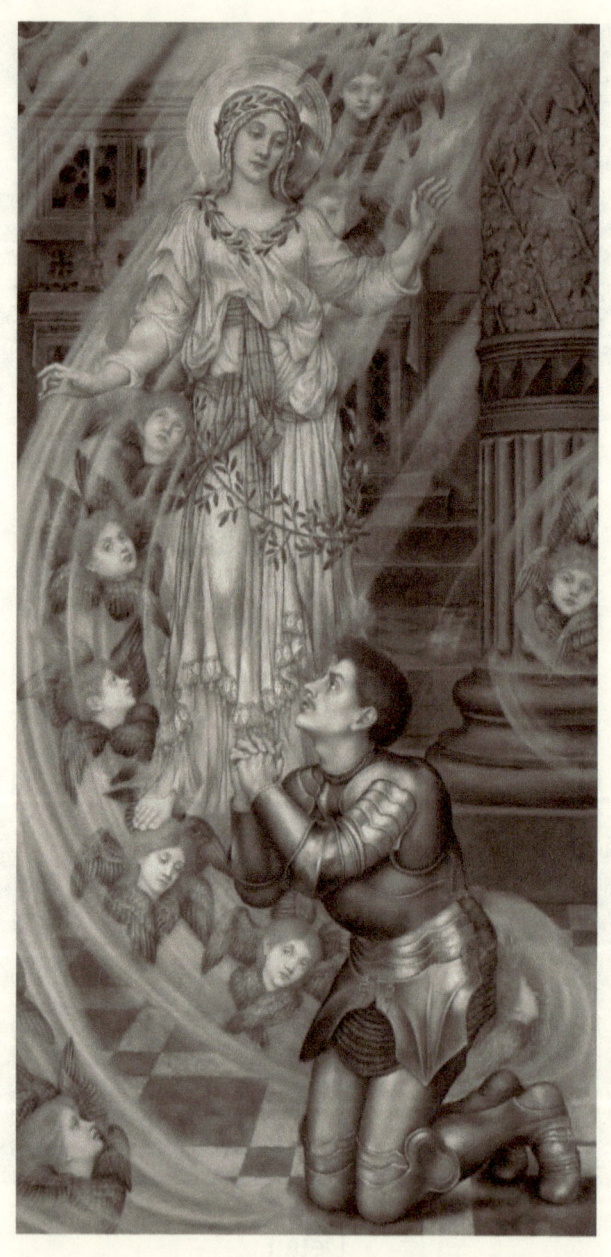

Our Lady of Peace (c. 1902)
Oil on canvas

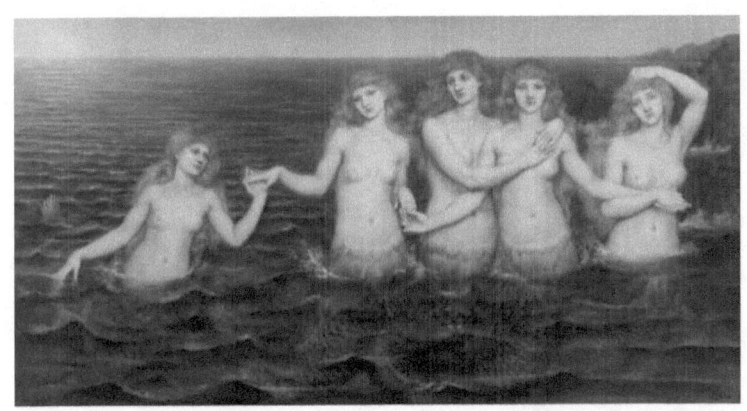

The Sea Maidens (1885-1886)
Oil on canvas

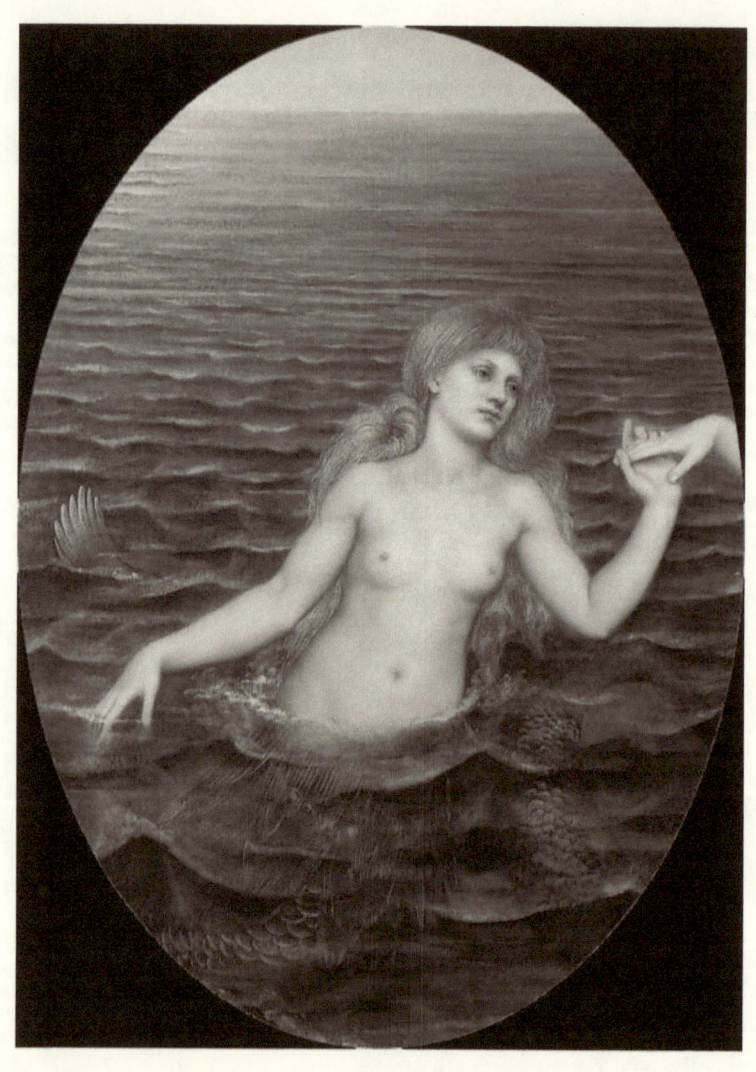

Detail

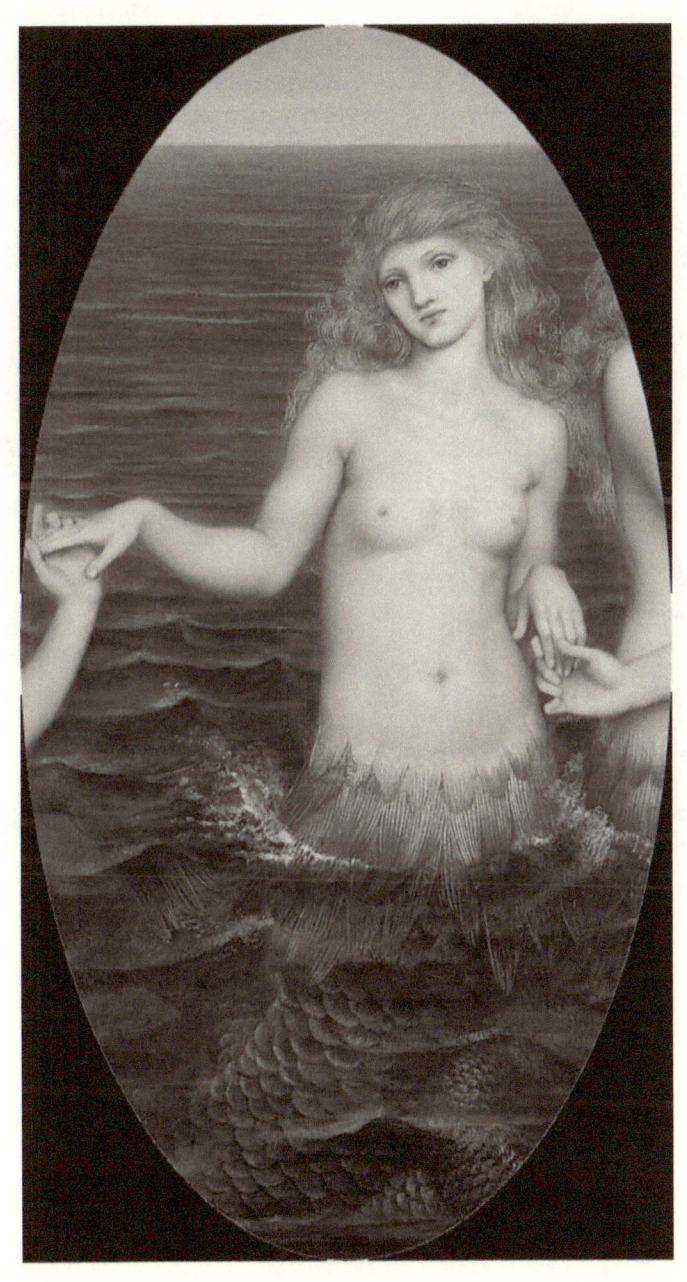

Detail

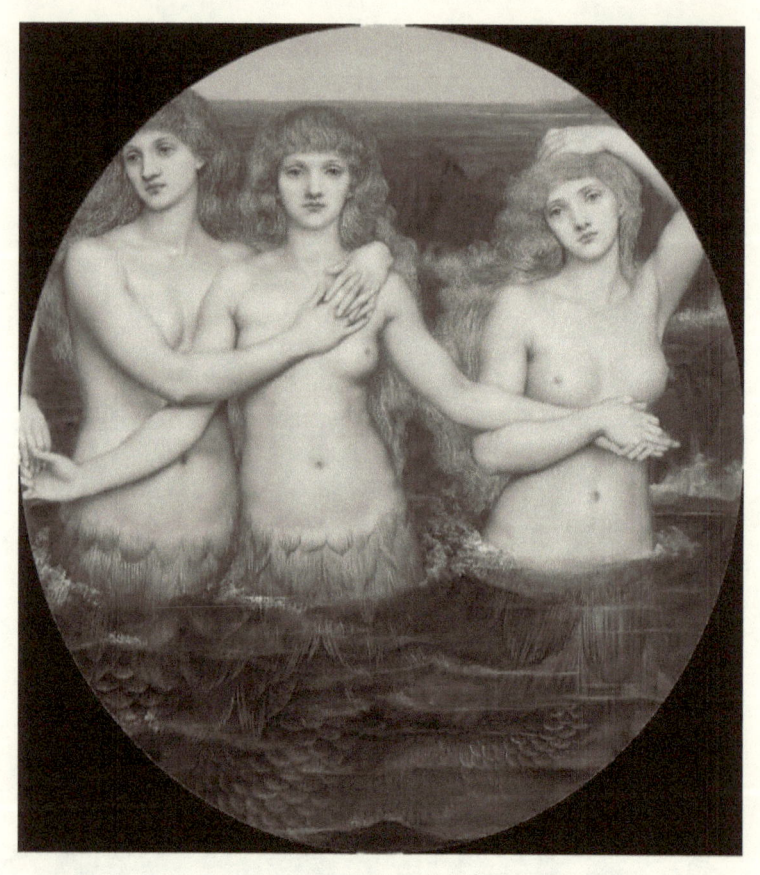

Detail

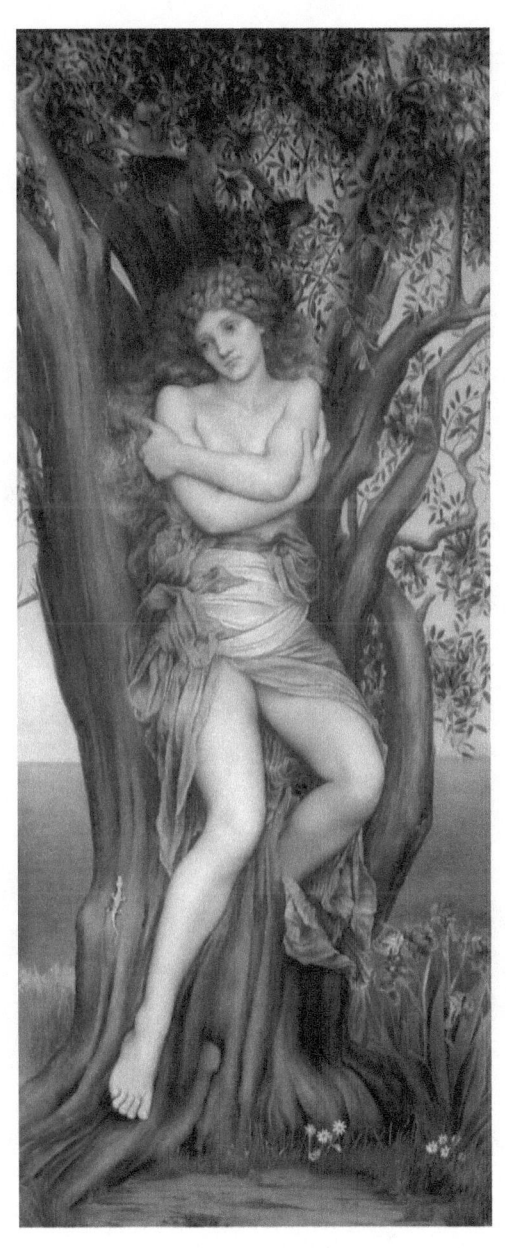

The Dryad (1884-1885)
Oil on canvas

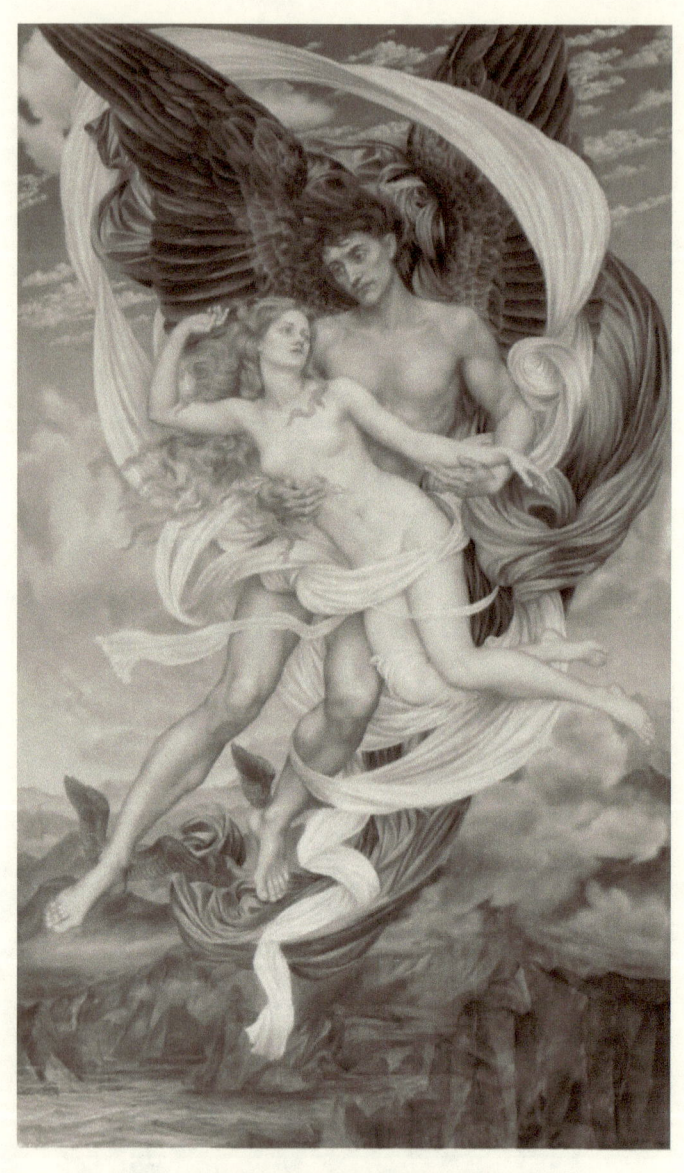

Boreas and Orietyia
Oil on canvas

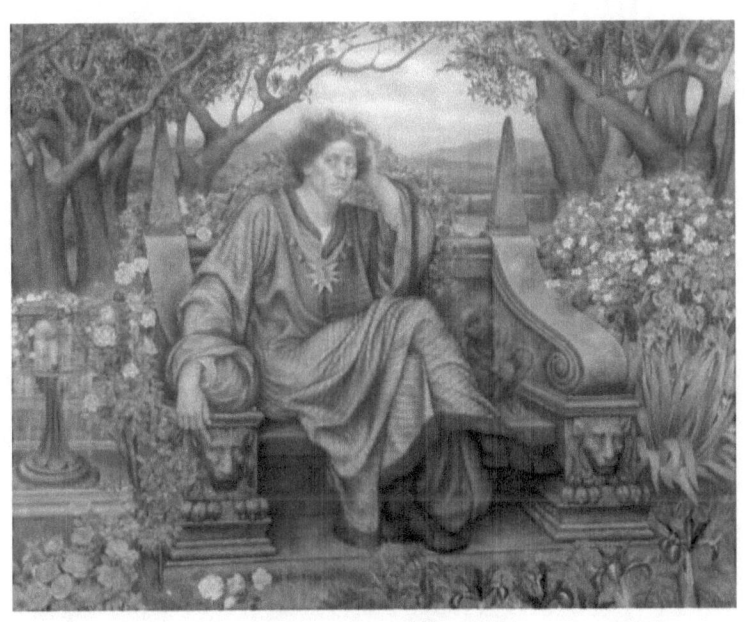

A Soul in Hell
Oil on canvas

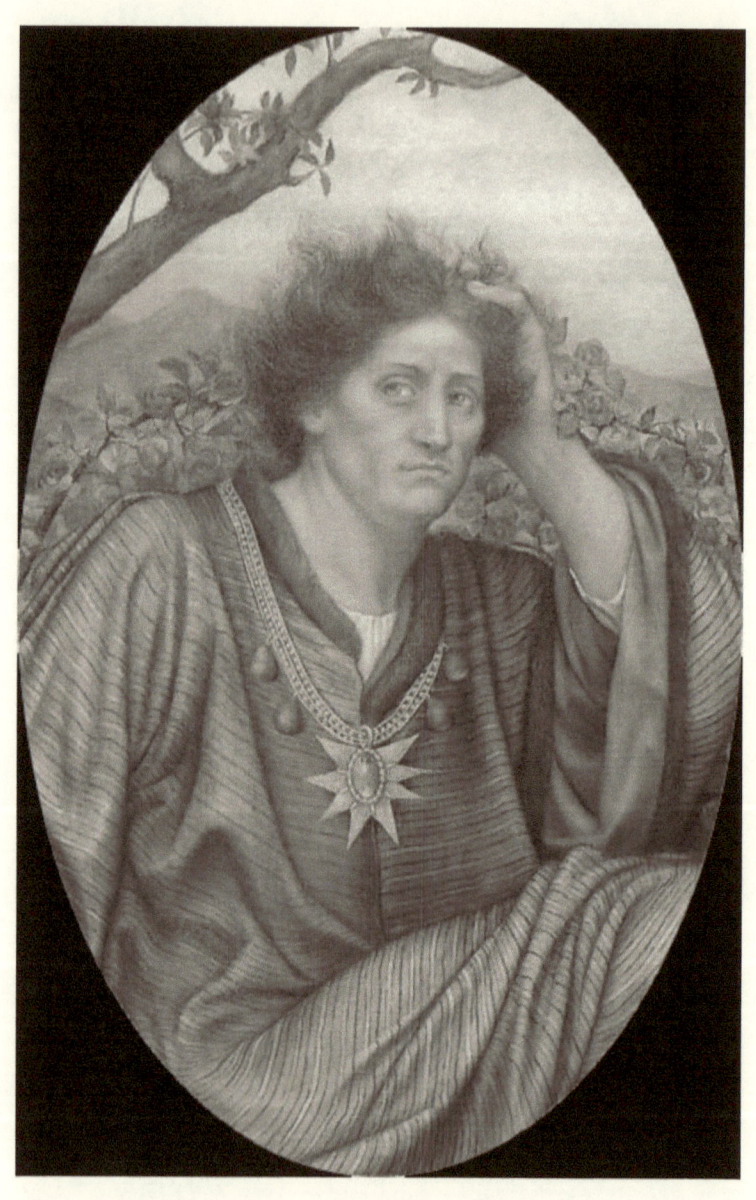

Detail

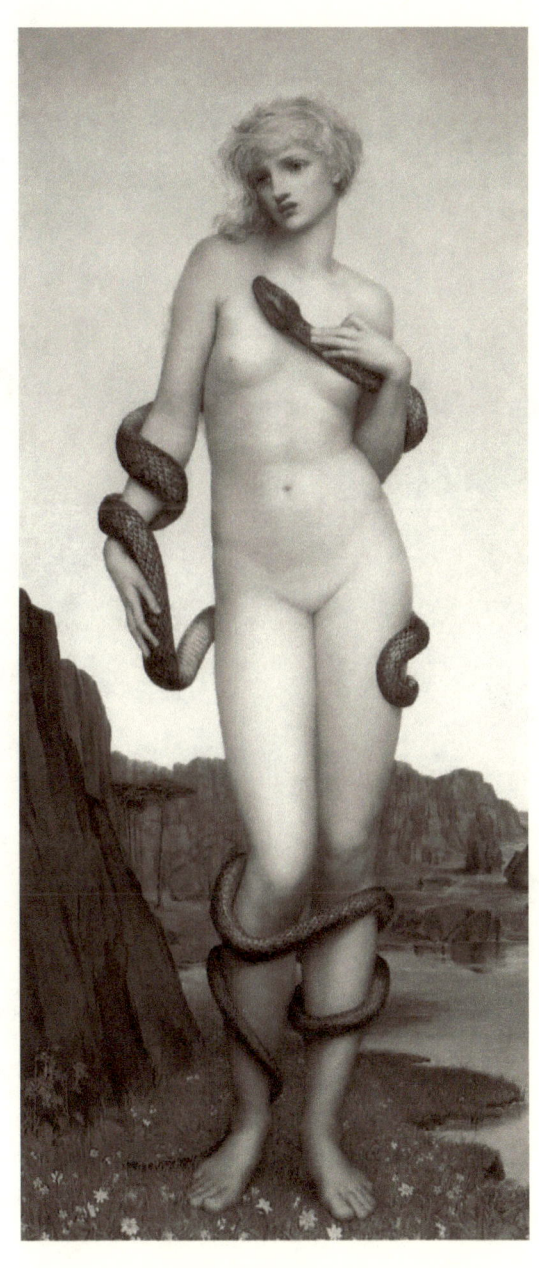

Cadmus and Harmonia (1877)
Oil on canvas

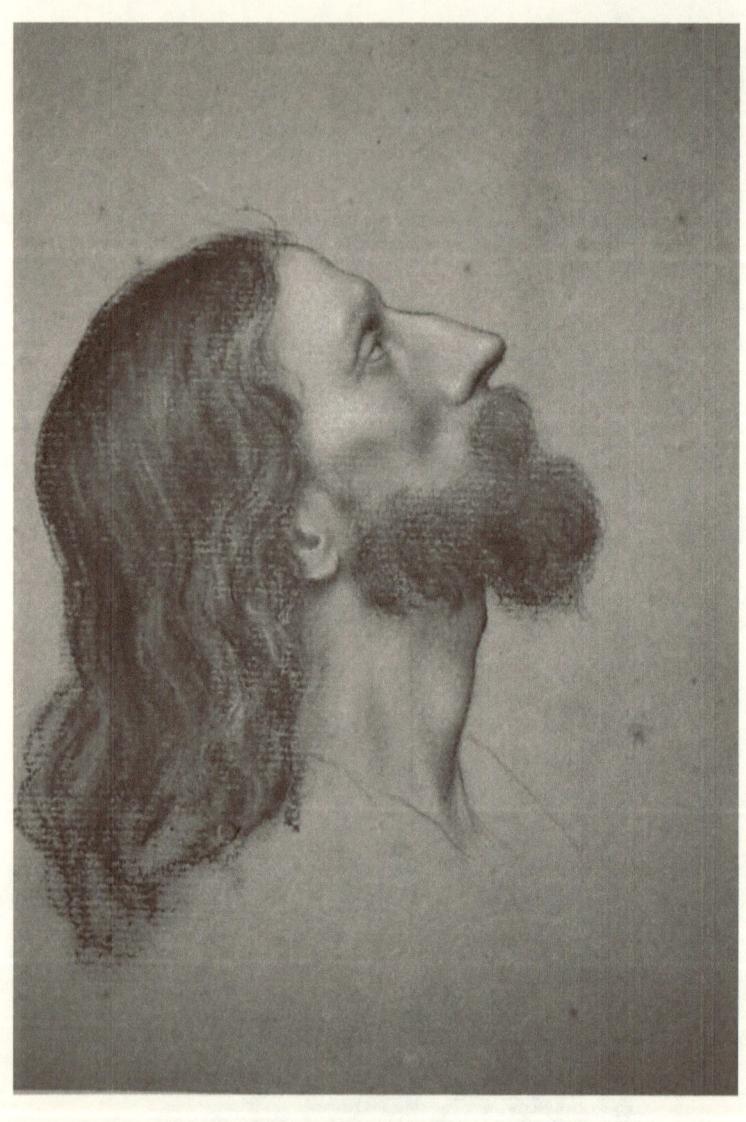

Study for "St. Christina Giving her Father's Jewels to
the Poor", 1904

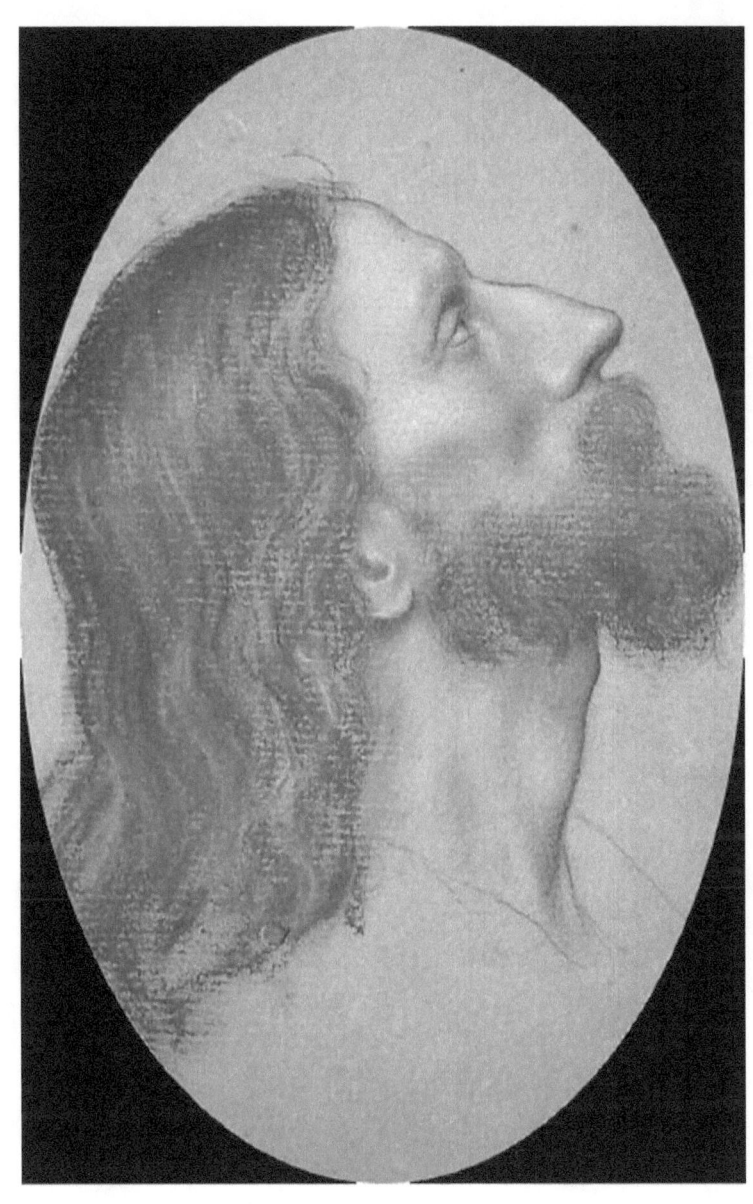

Detail

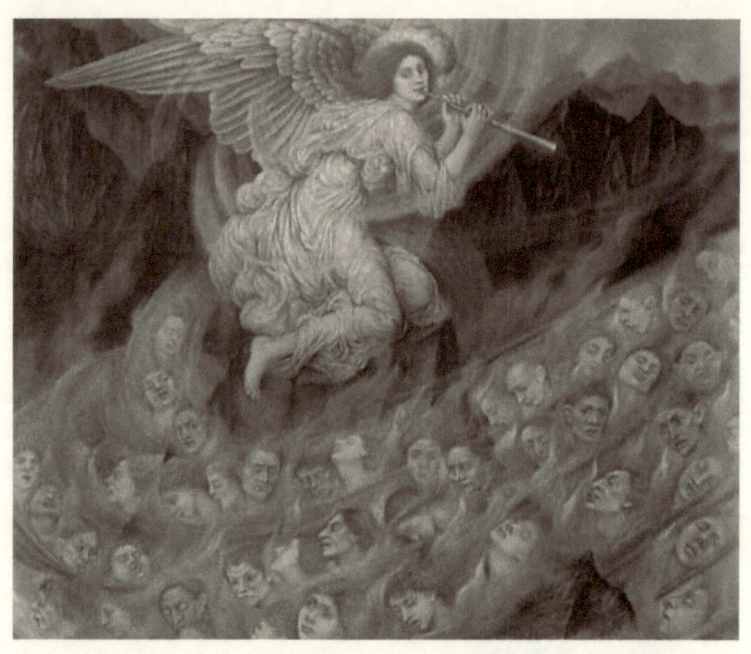

An Angel Piping to the Souls in Hell (1916)
Oil on canvas

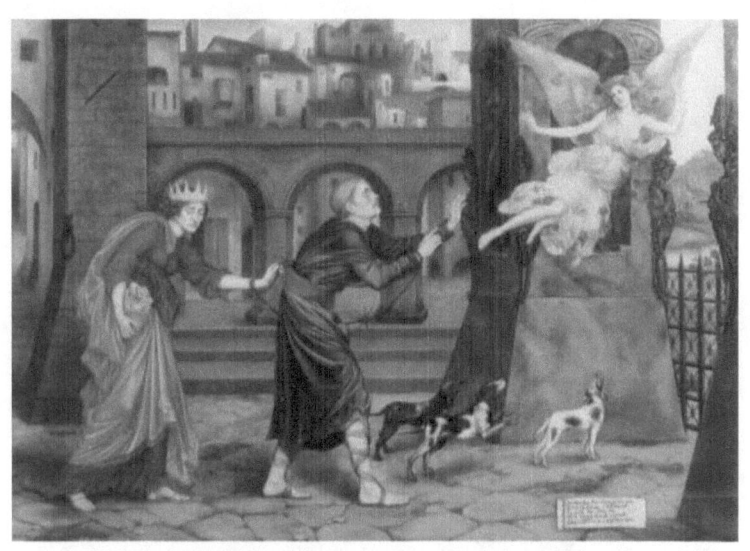

Blindness and Cupidity Chasing Joy from the City
(1897), Oil on canvas

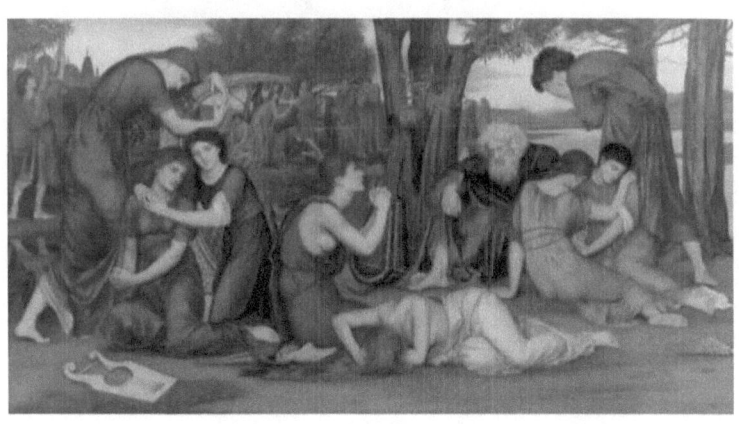

By the Waters of Babylon (1882-1883)
Oil on canvas

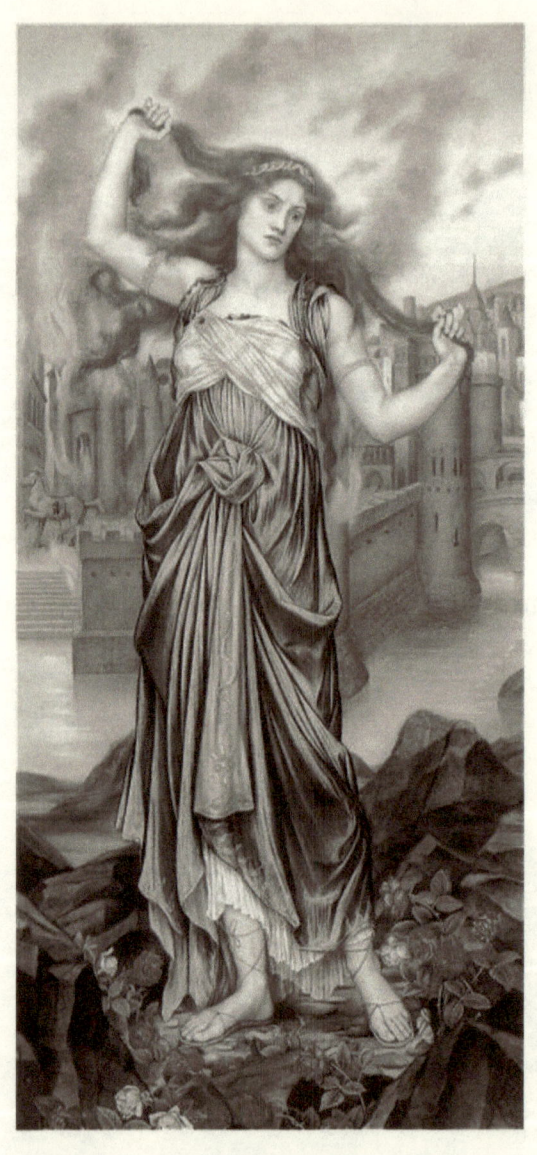

Cassandra (1898)
Oil on canvas

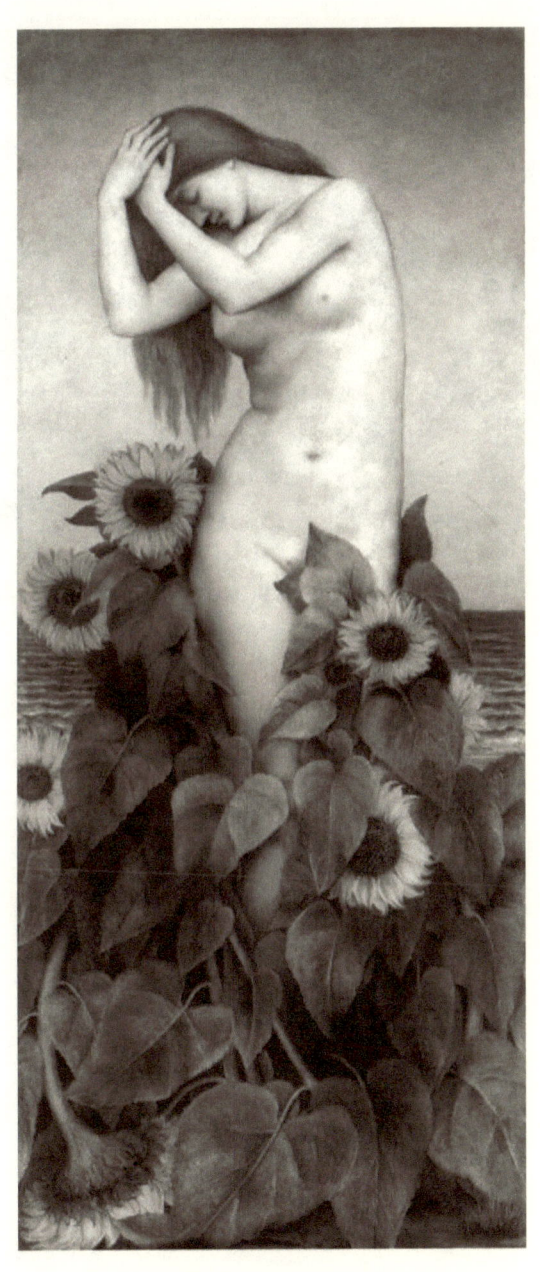

Clytie (1886-1887)
Oil on canvas

43

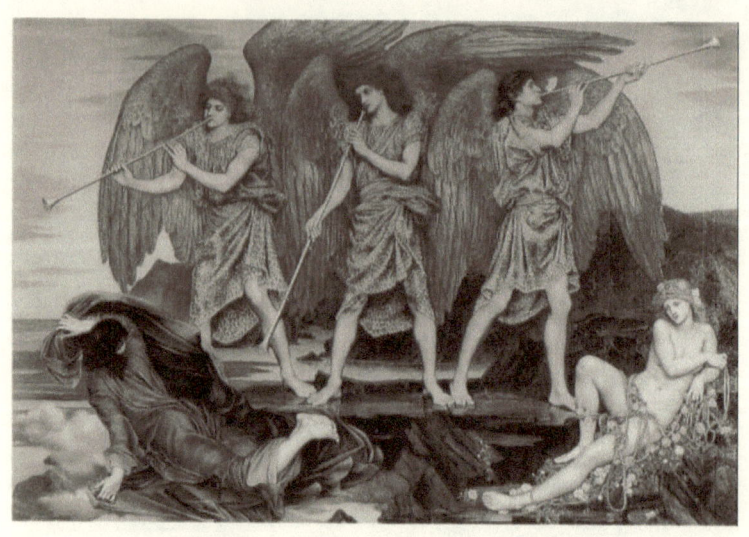

Dawn / Aurora Triumphans (1886)
Oil on canvas

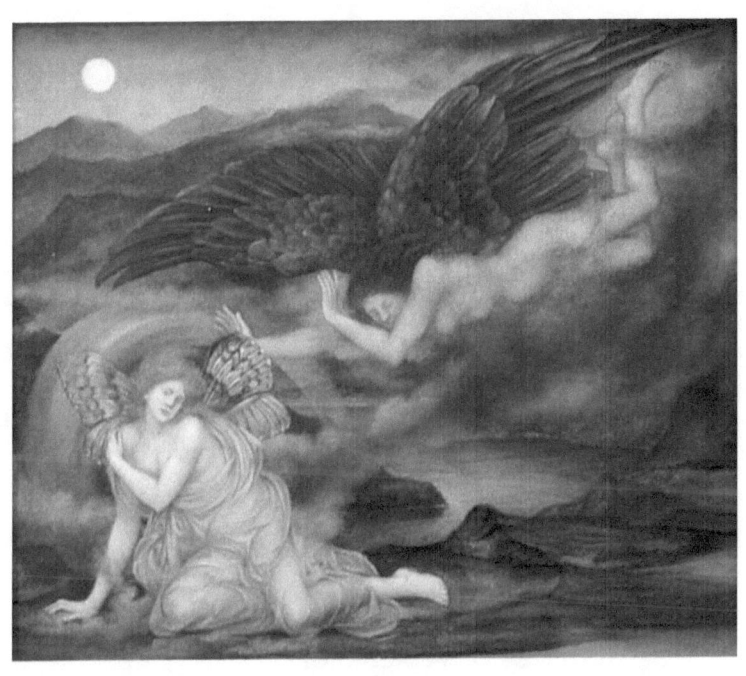

Death of a Butterfly (c. 1905-1910)
Watercolor

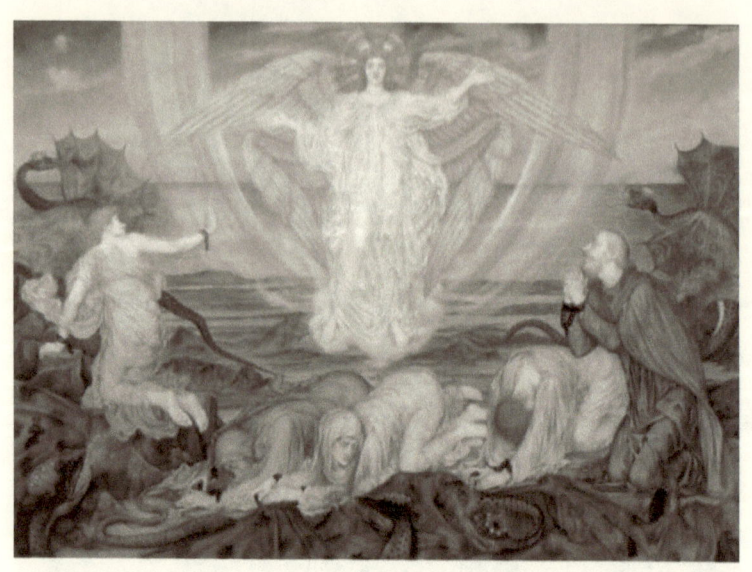

Death of the Dragon (1914)
Watercolor

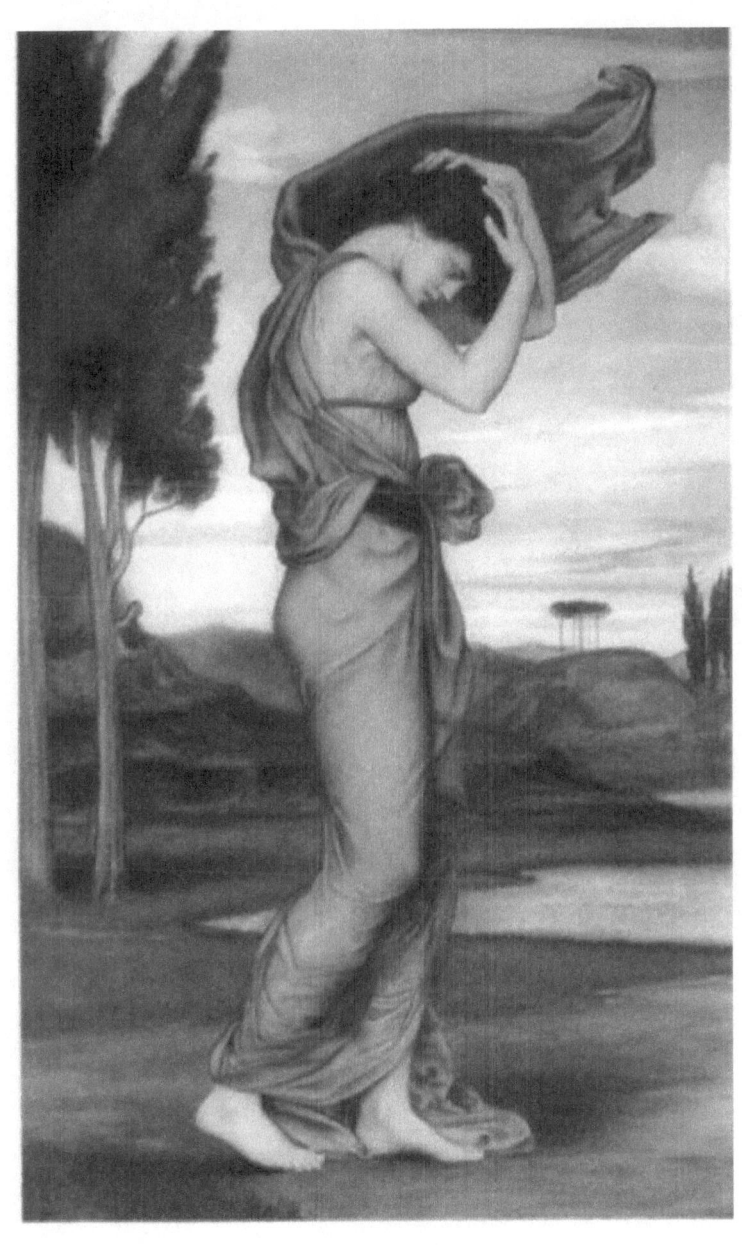

Deianera
Oil on canvas

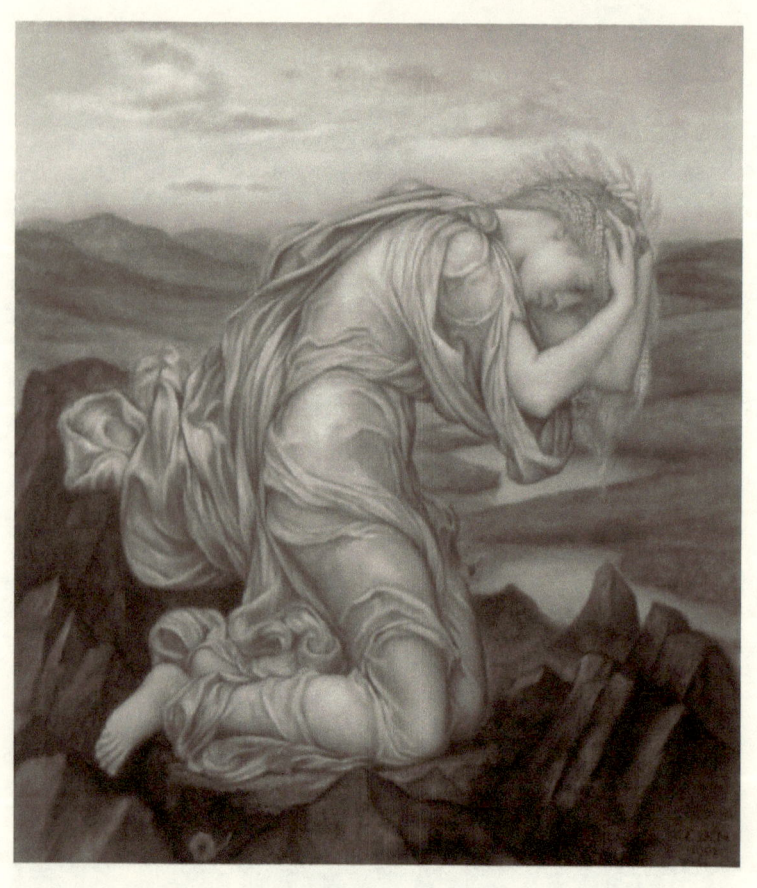

Demeter Mourning for Persephone (1906)
Oil on canvas

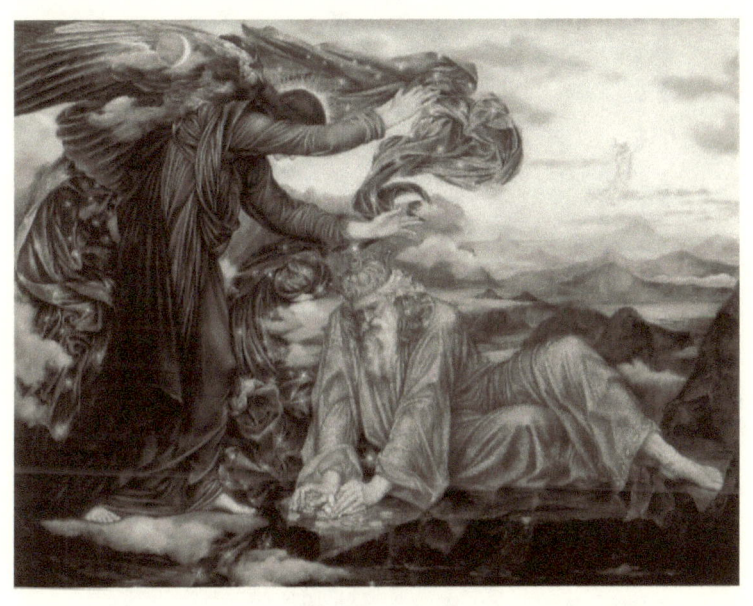

Earthbound (1897), Oil on canvas

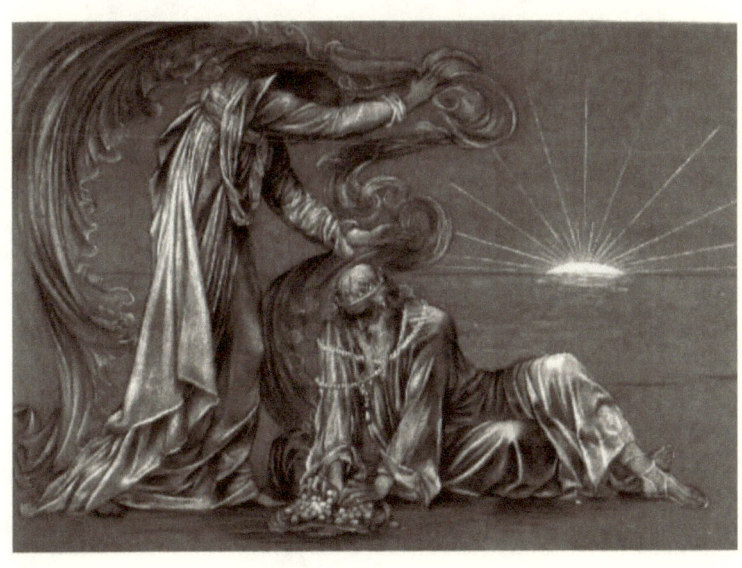

Earthbound, study (1897)

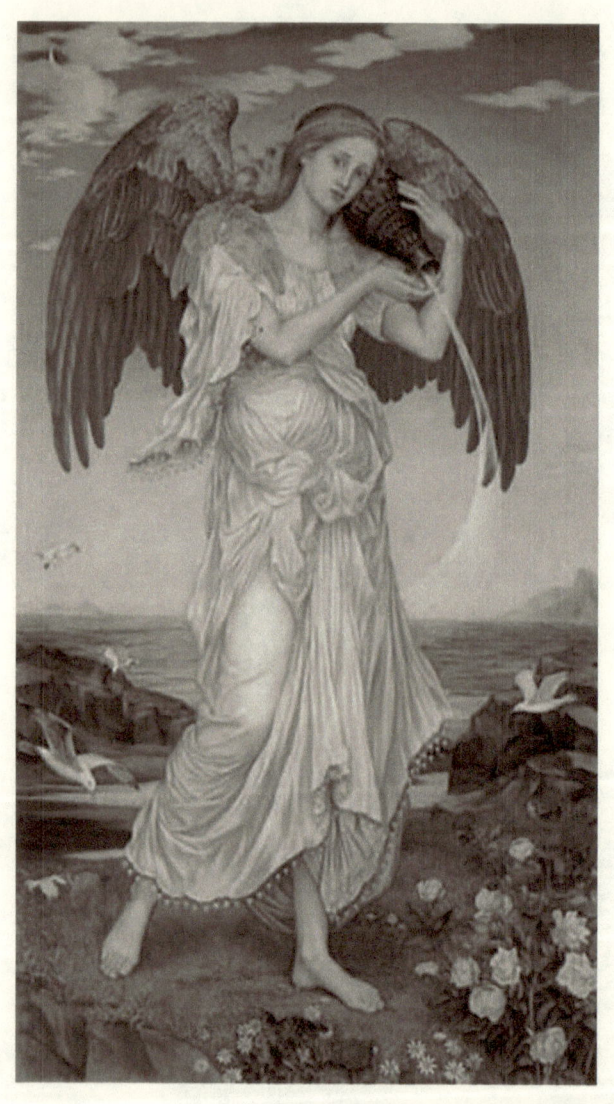

Eos (1895)
Oil on canvas

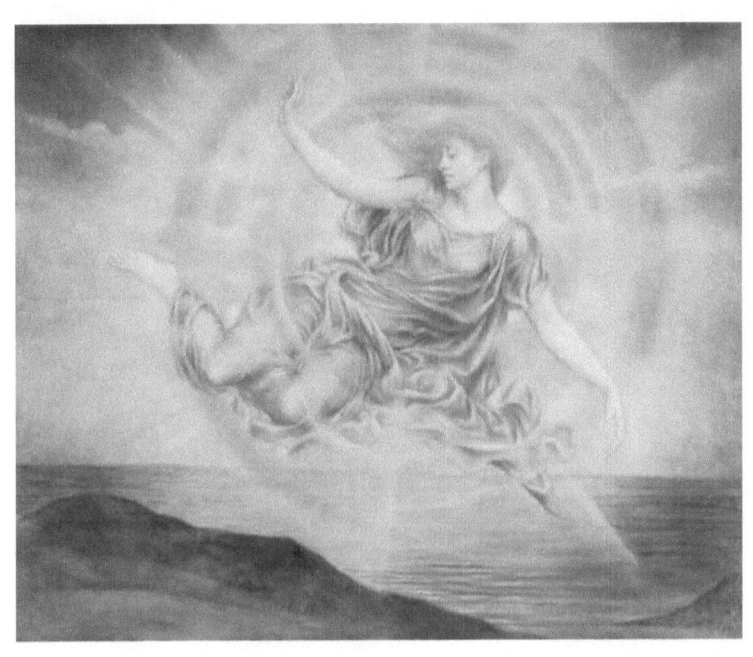

Evening Star over the Sea
Watercolor

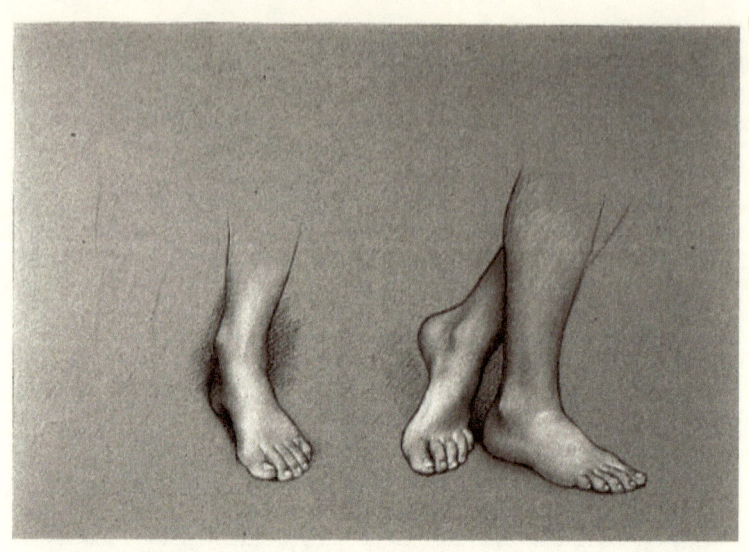

Feet, study
Pastel

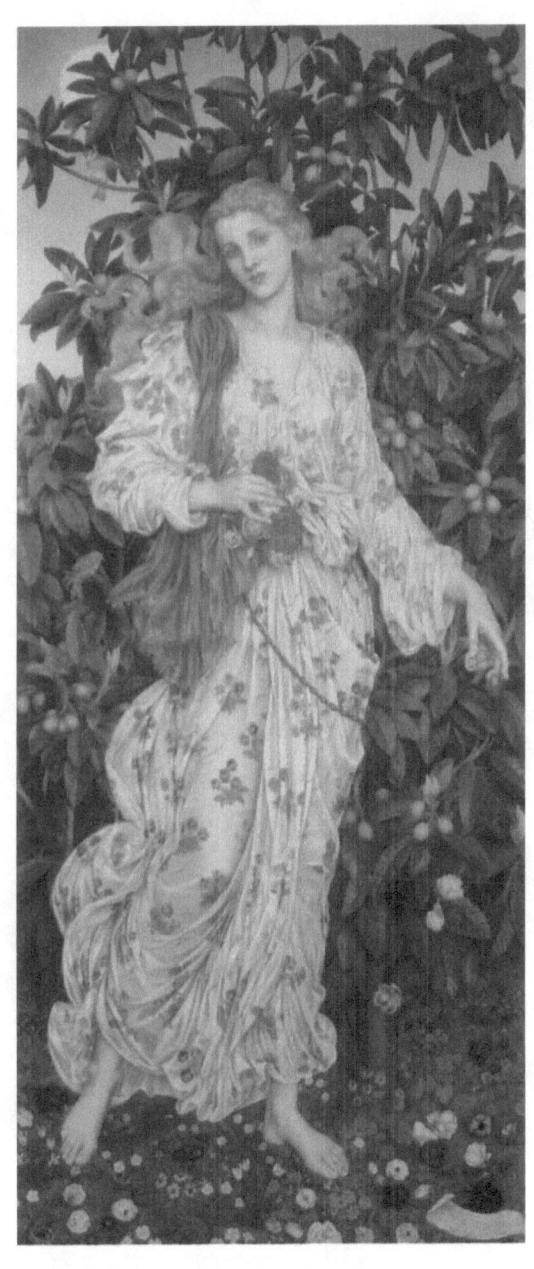

Flora (1894)
Oil on canvas

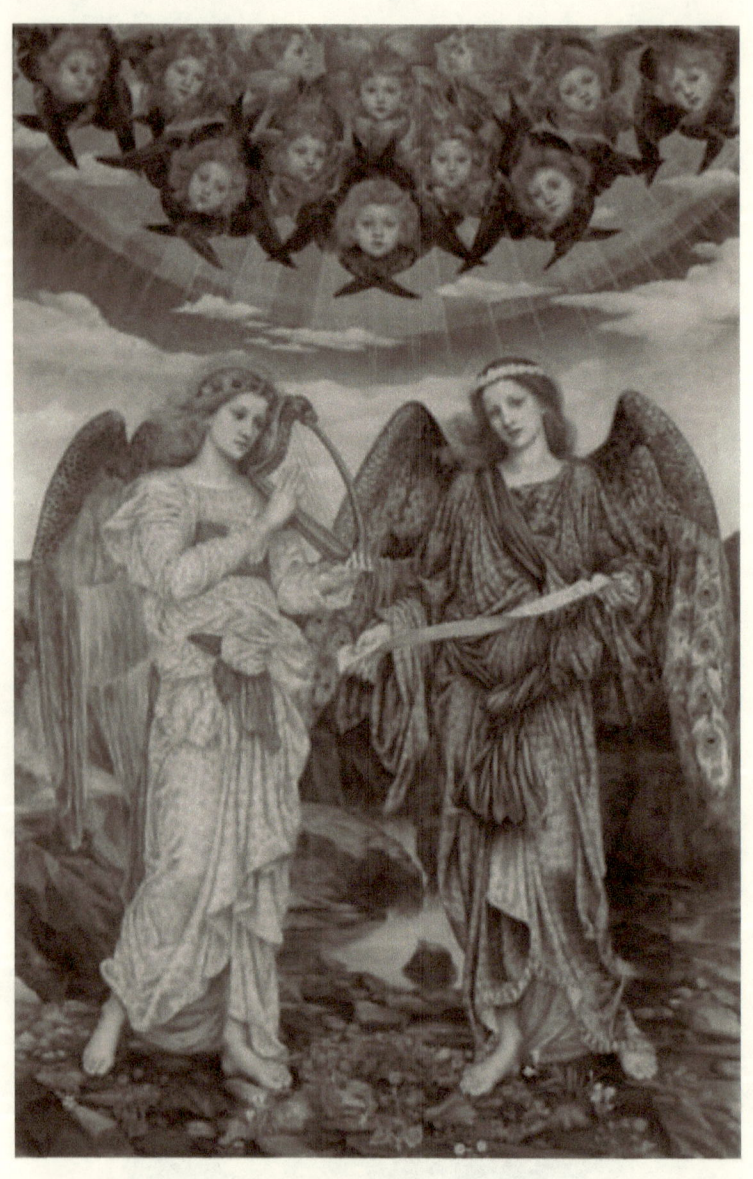

Gloria in Excelsis (1893)
Oil on canvas

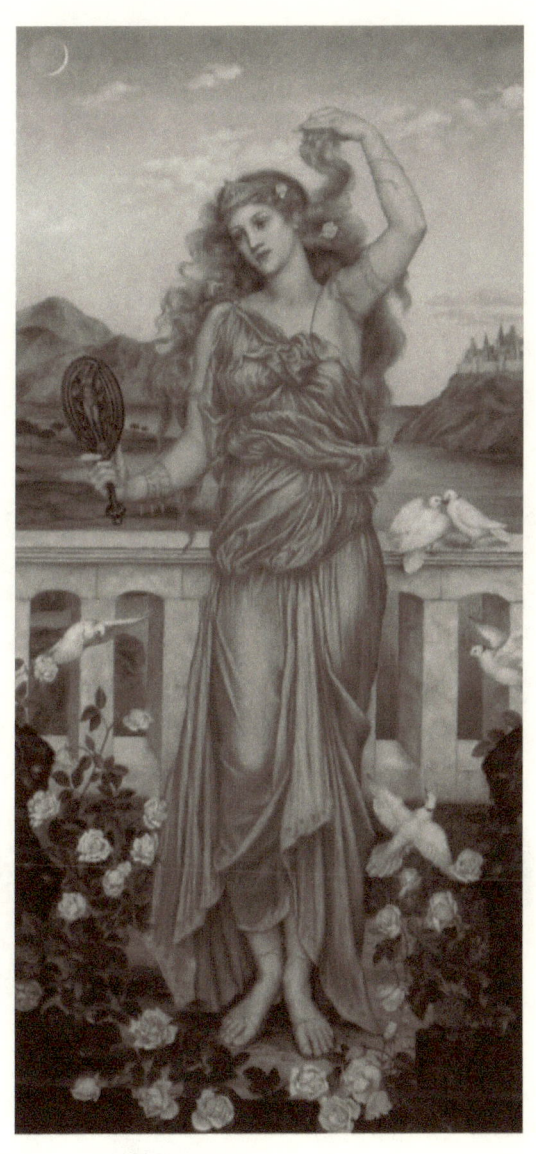

Helen of Troy
Oil on canvas

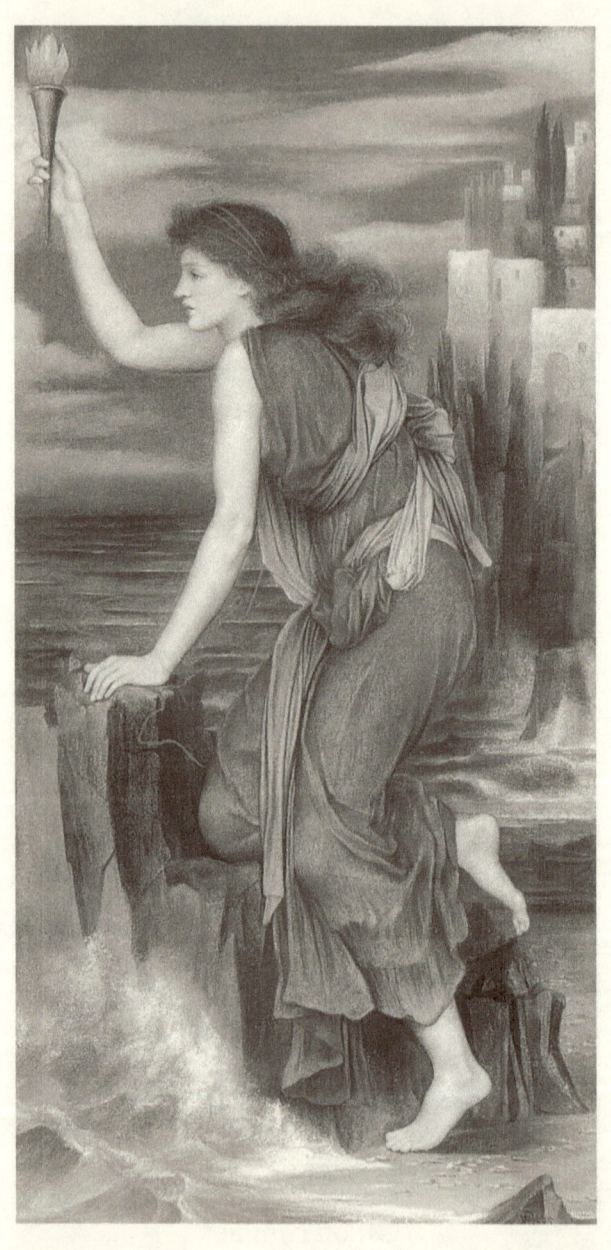

Hero Awaiting the Return of Leander (1885)
Pastel

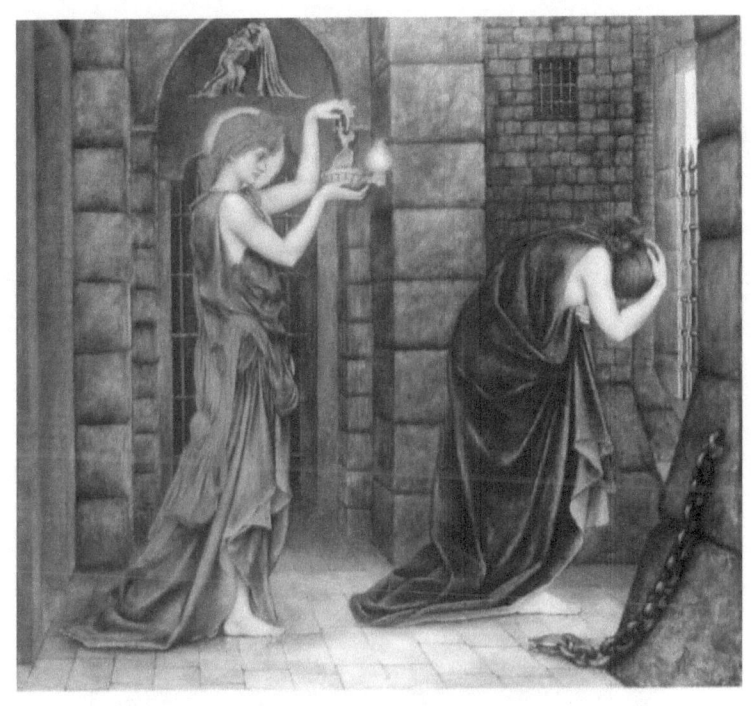

Hope in the Prison of Despair (1887)
Oil on canvas

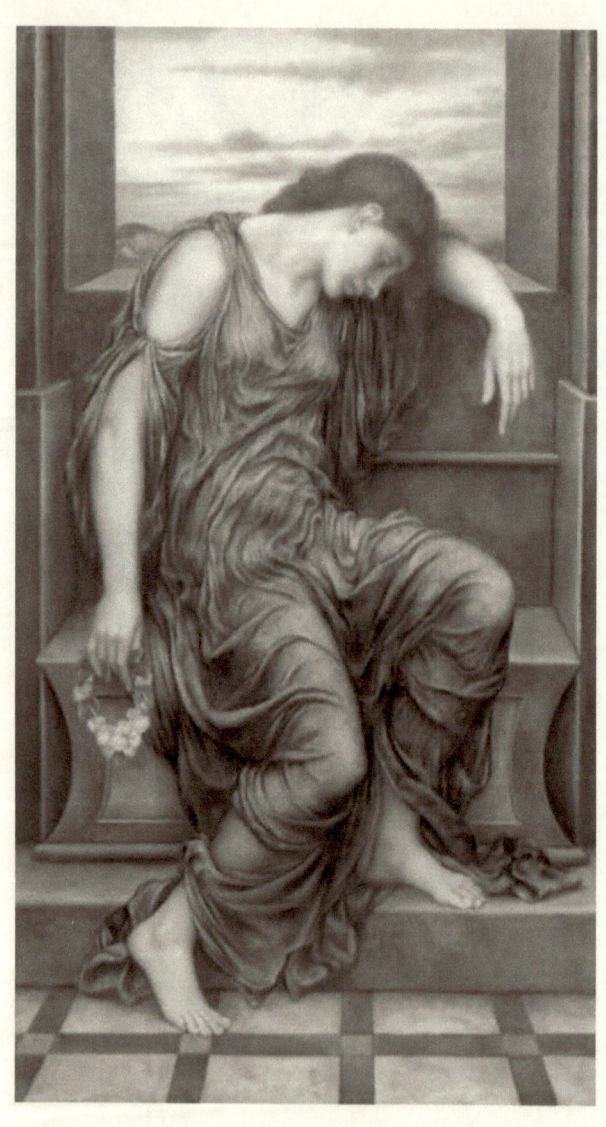

In Memoriam
Oil on canvas

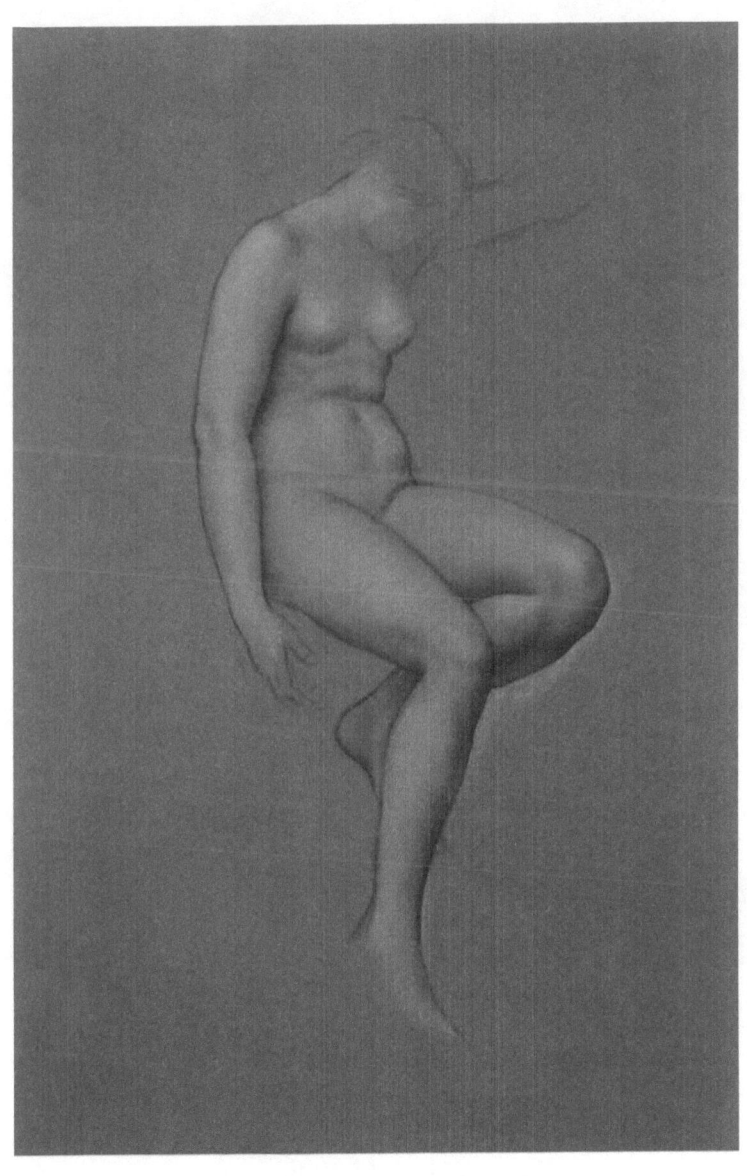

In Memoriam, study (1898)
Pastel

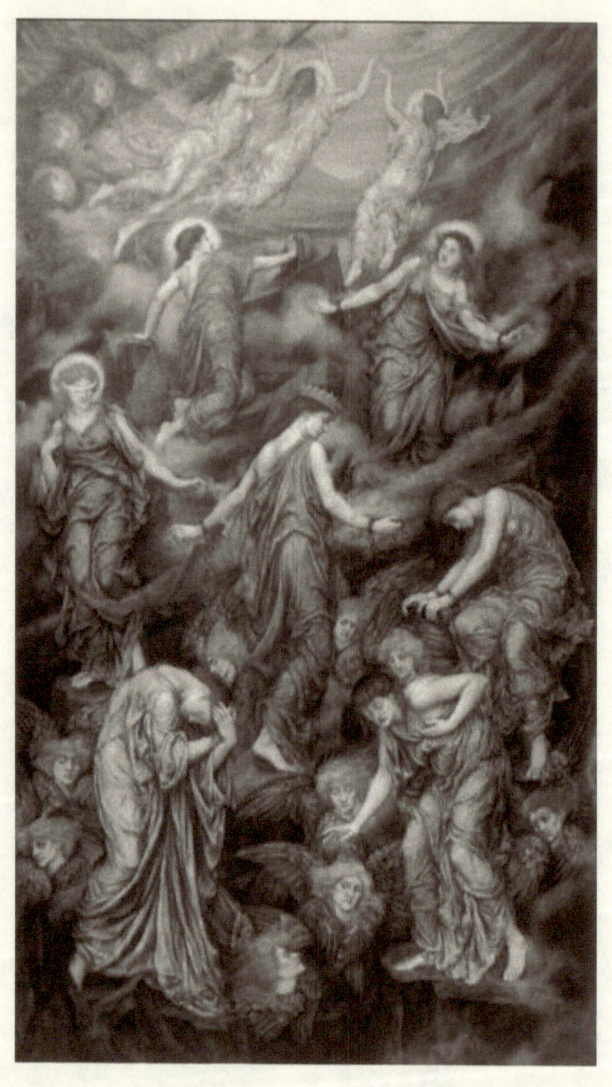

Kingdom of Heaven
Oil on canvas

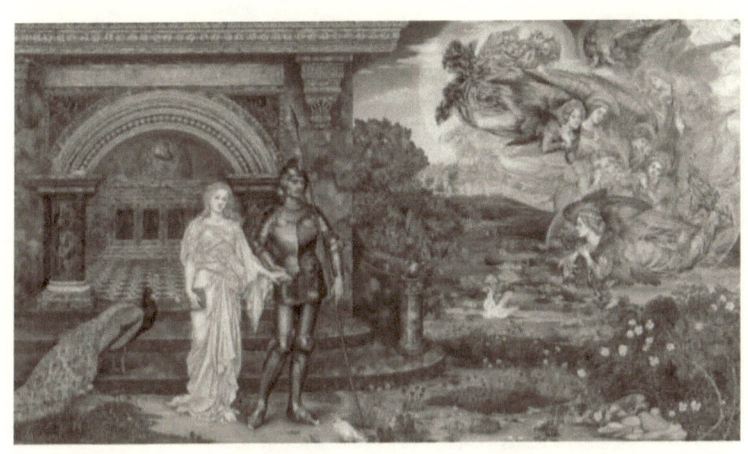

Life and Thought Have Gone Away (1893)
Oil on canvas

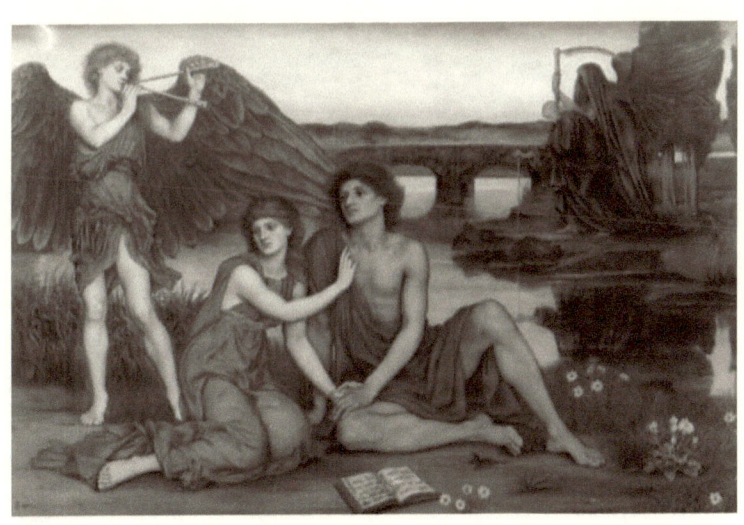

Love's Passing (1883-1884)
Oil on canvas

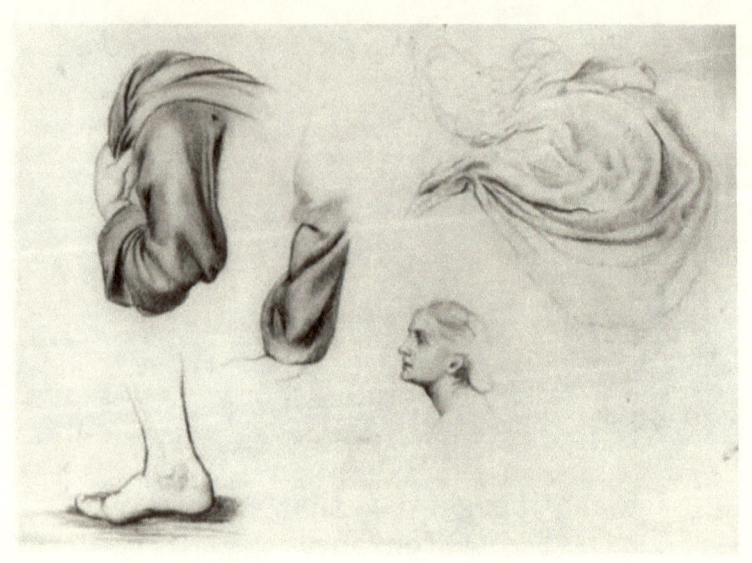

Love's Passing, study (1883)
Pencil

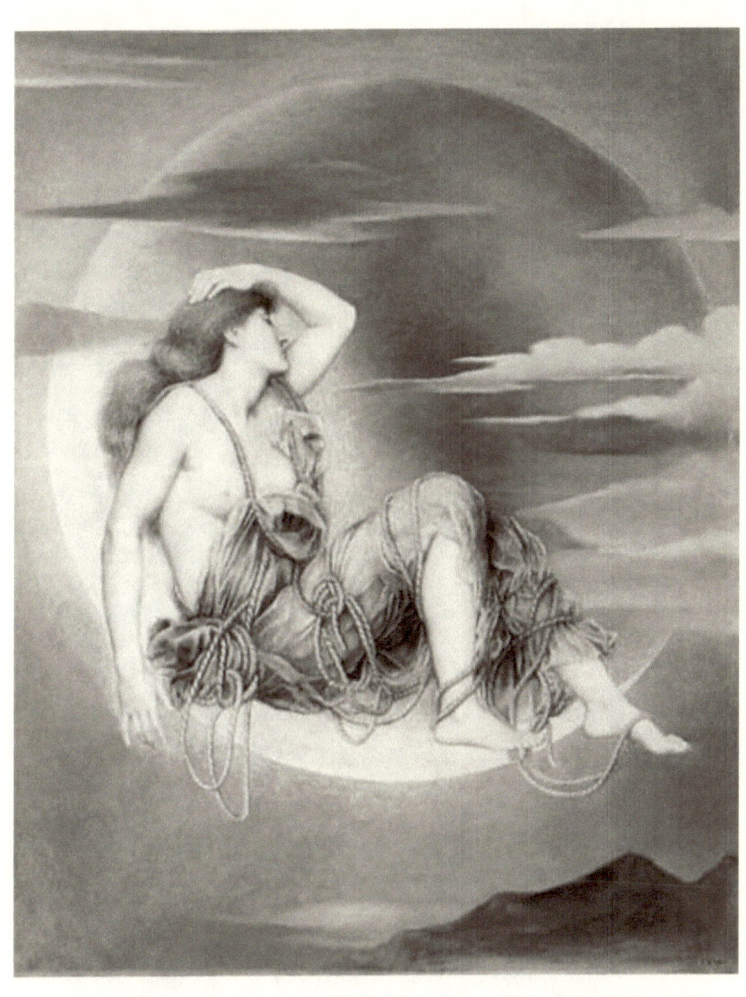

Luna (1885)
Oil on canvas

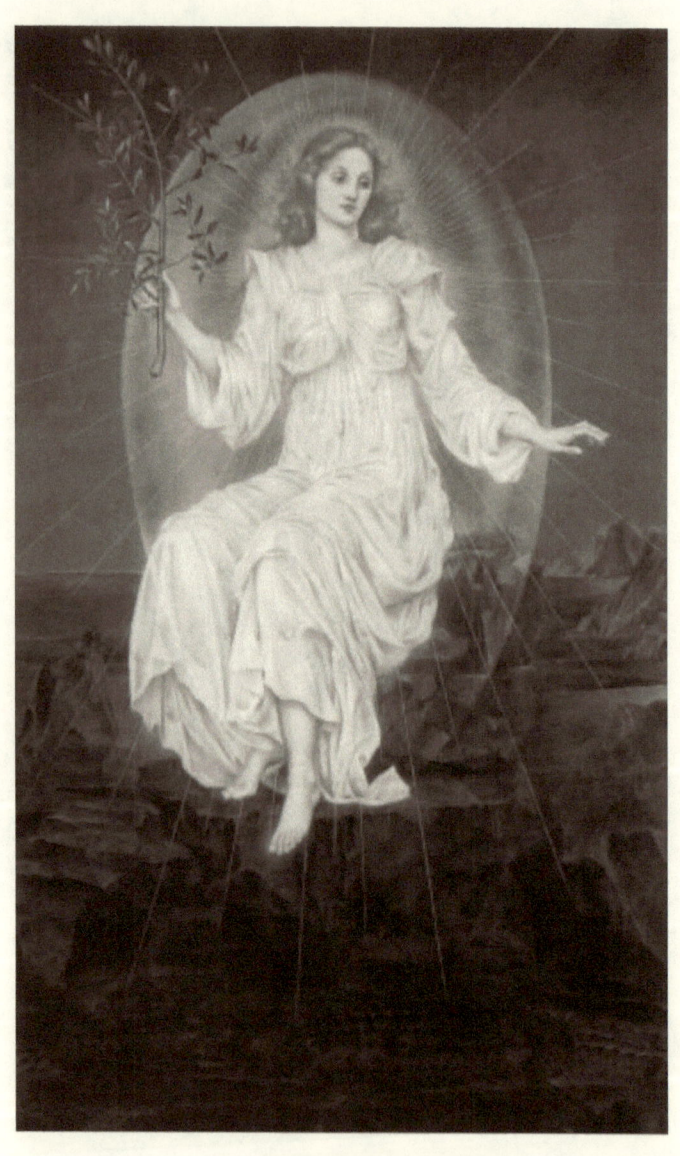

Lux in Tenebris (1895)
Oil on canvas

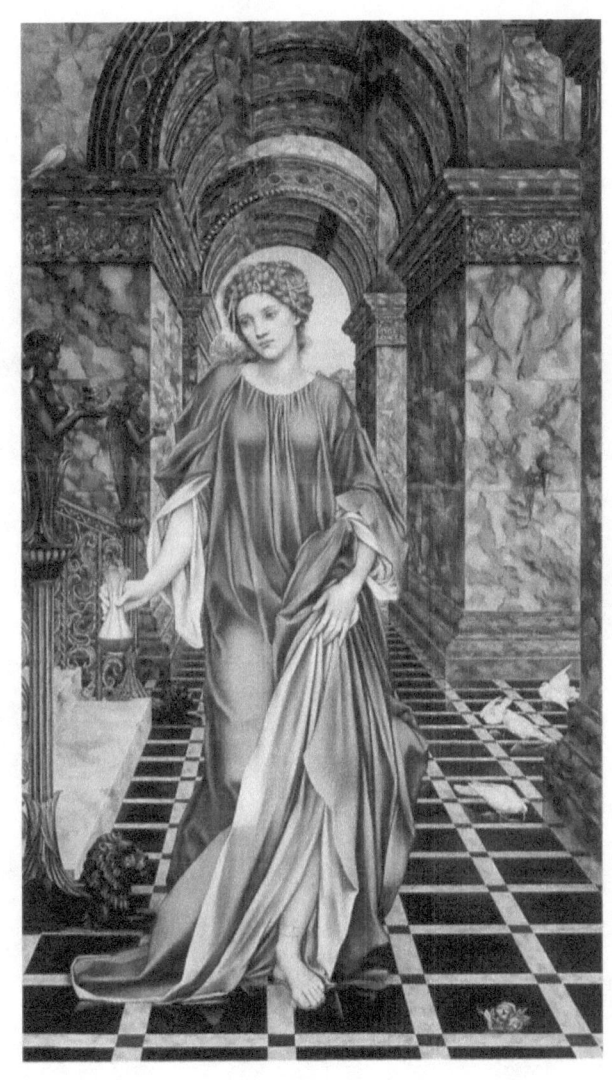

Medea (1889)
Oil on canvas

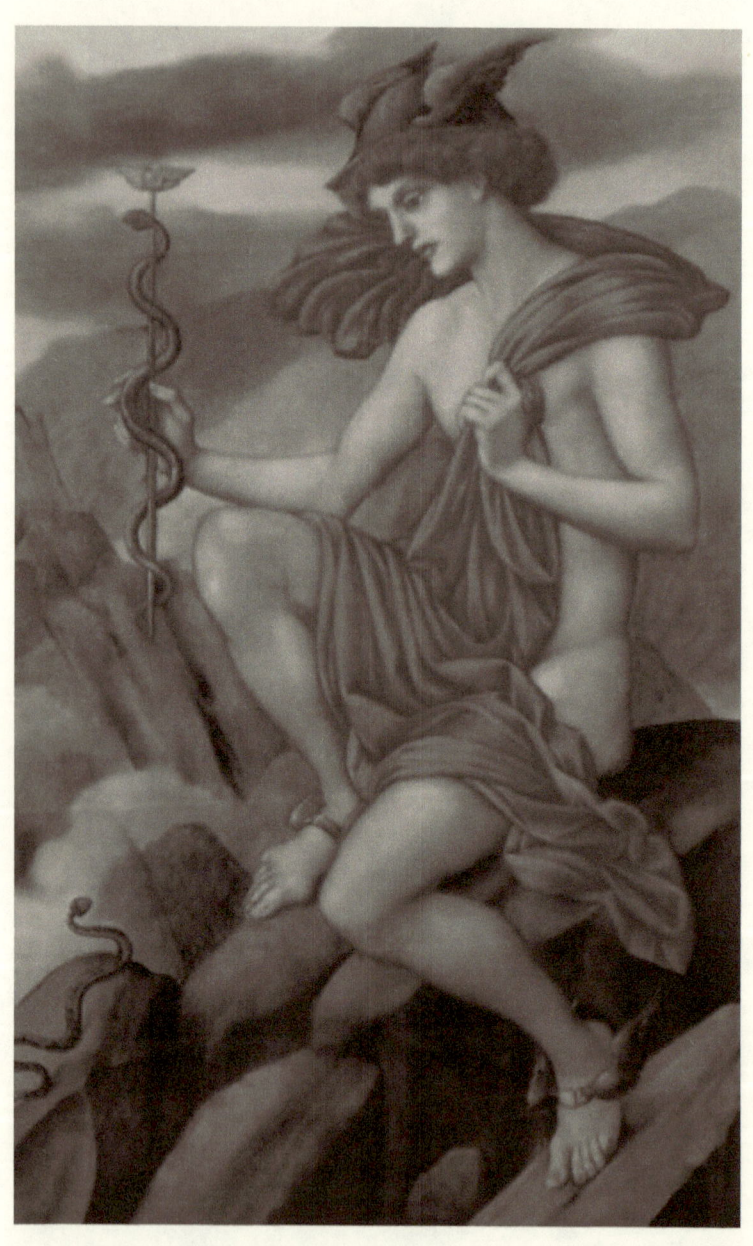

Mercury
Oil on canvas

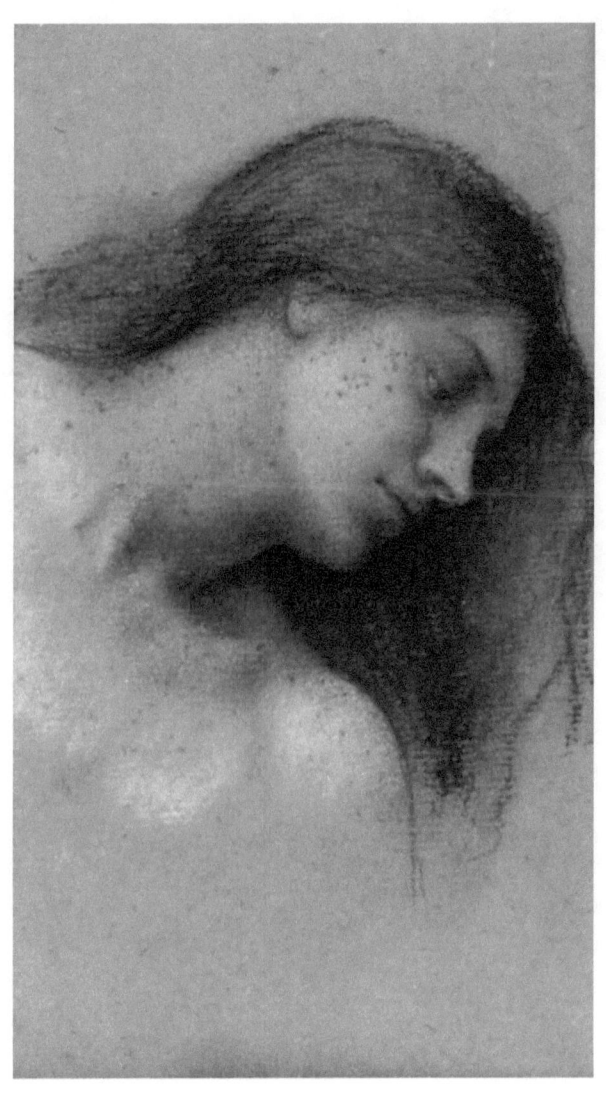

Moonbeans Dipping into the Ocean, study
Pastel

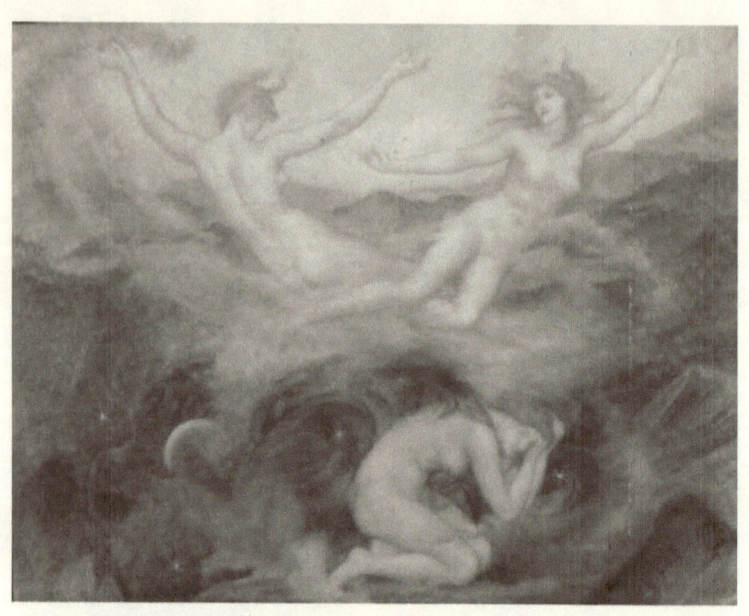

Night and Dawn
Watercolor

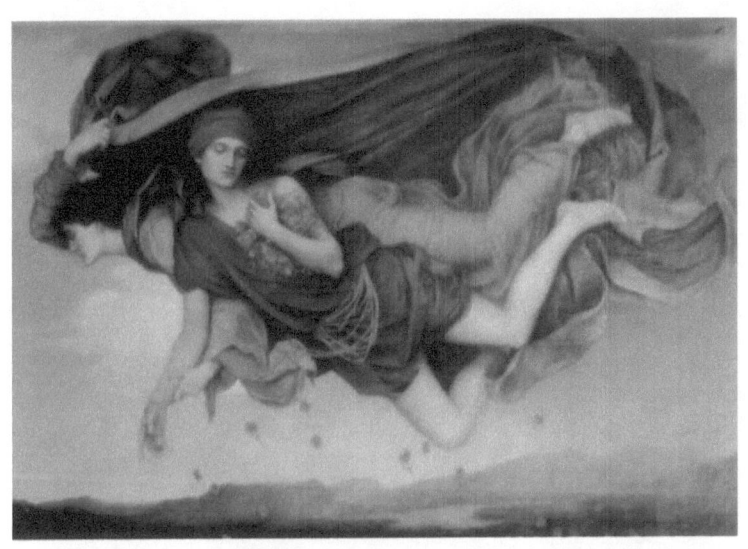

Night and Sleep (1878)
Oil on canvas

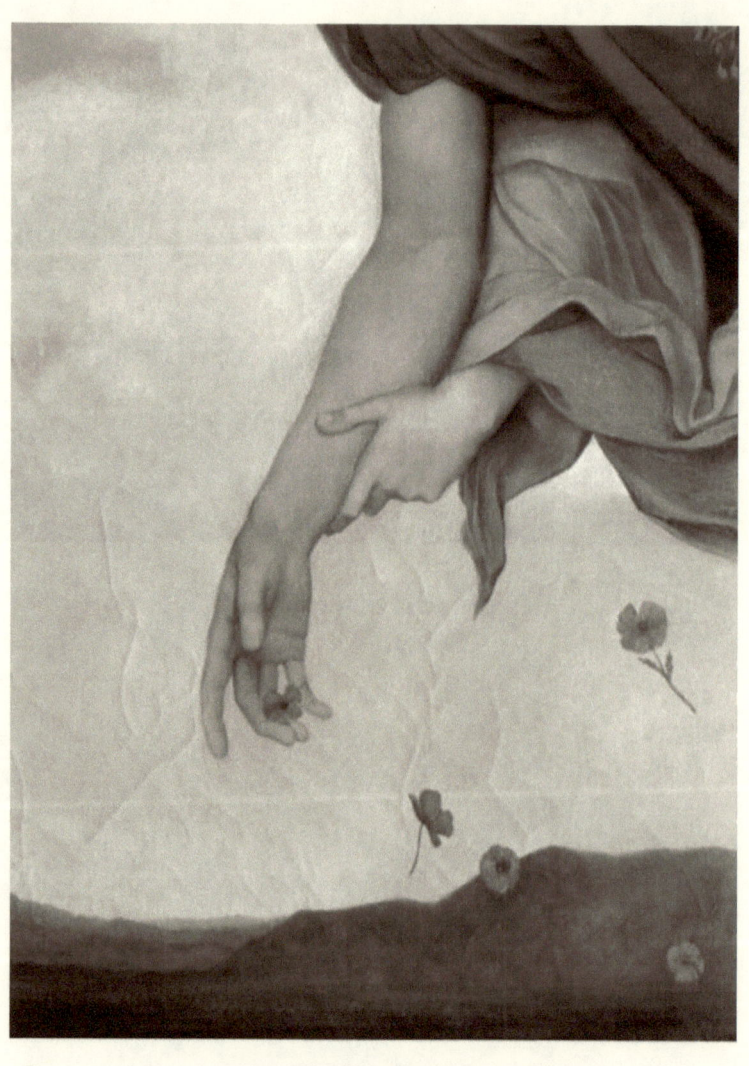

Night and Sleep, detail (1878)
Oil on canvas

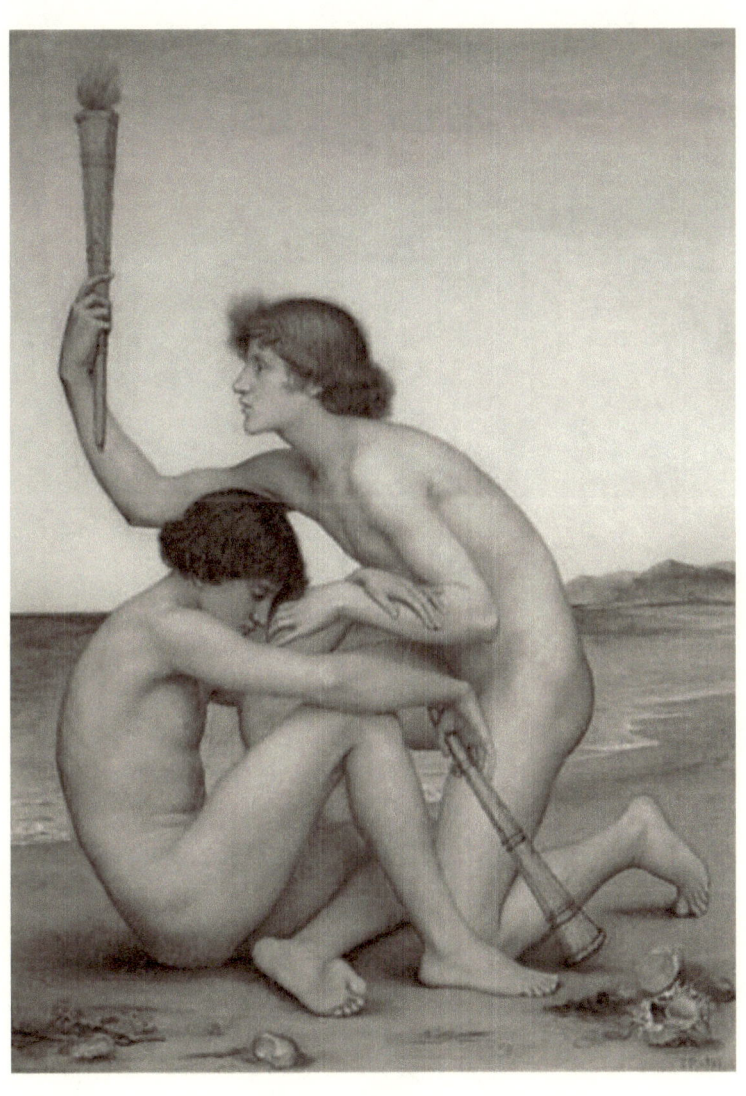

Phosphorus and Hesperus (1881)
Oil on canvas

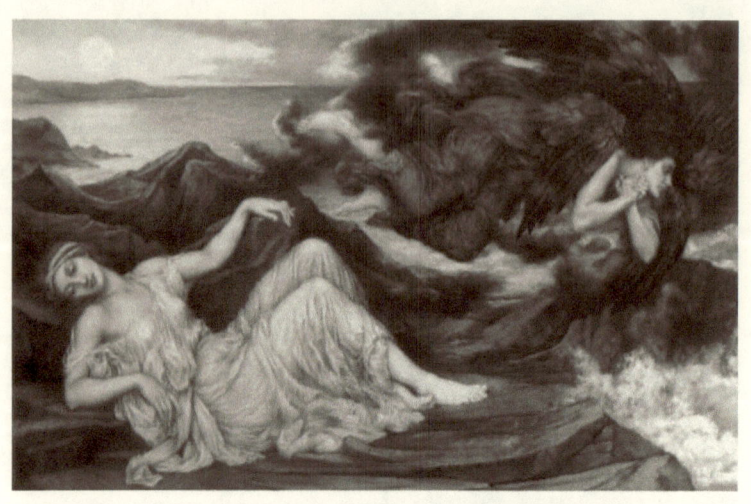

Port after Stormy Seas (1905)
Oil on canvas

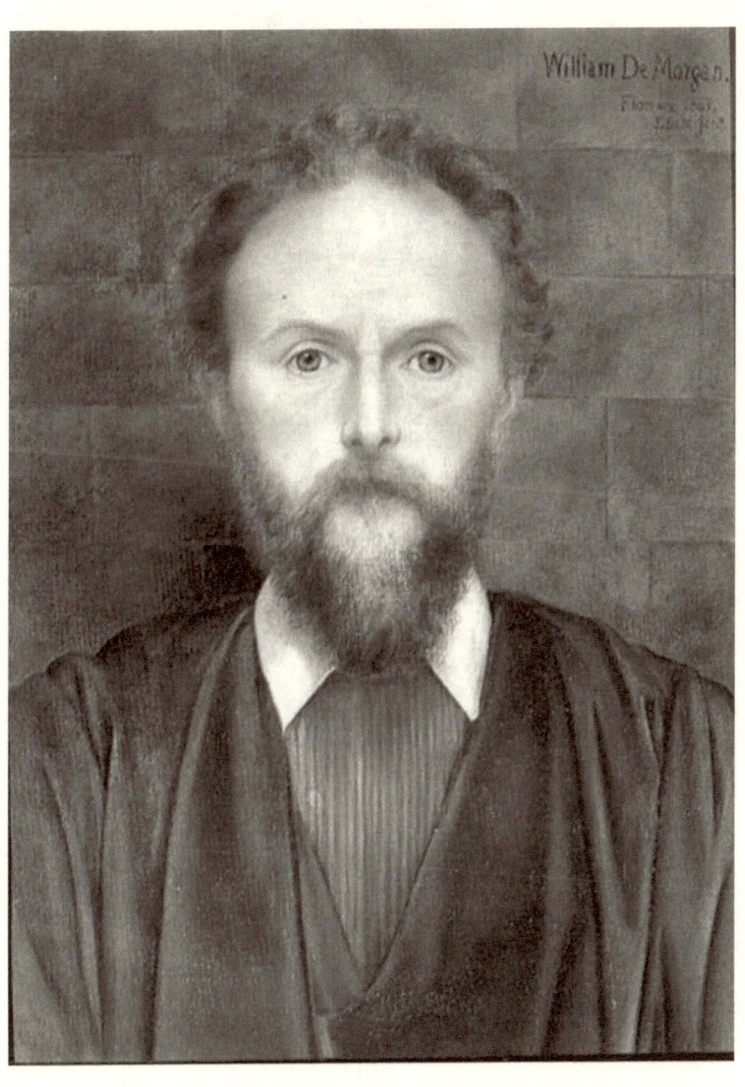

Portrait of William de Morgan (1893)
Oil on canvas

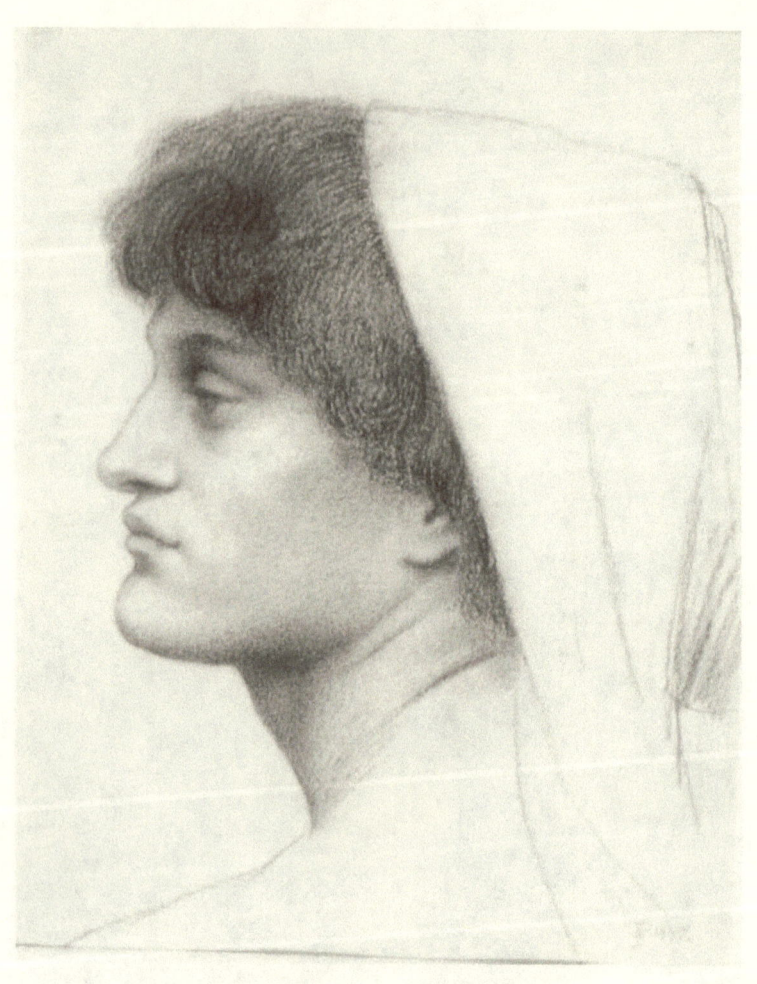

Profile of a Female Head (1885)
Pencil

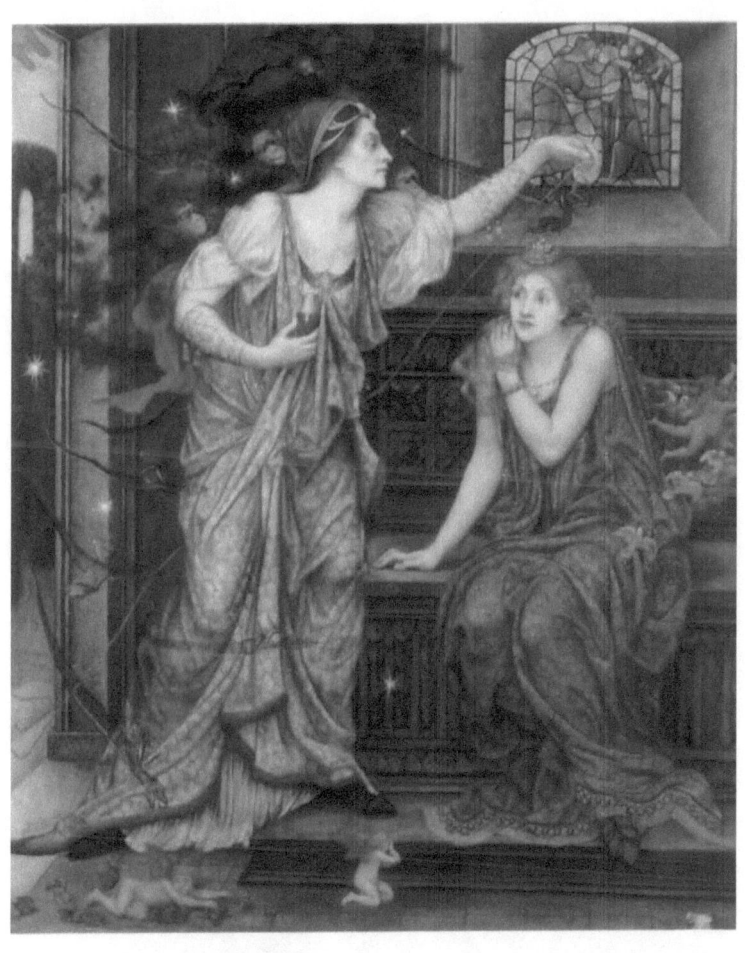

Queen Eleanor and Fair Rosamund
Oil on canvas

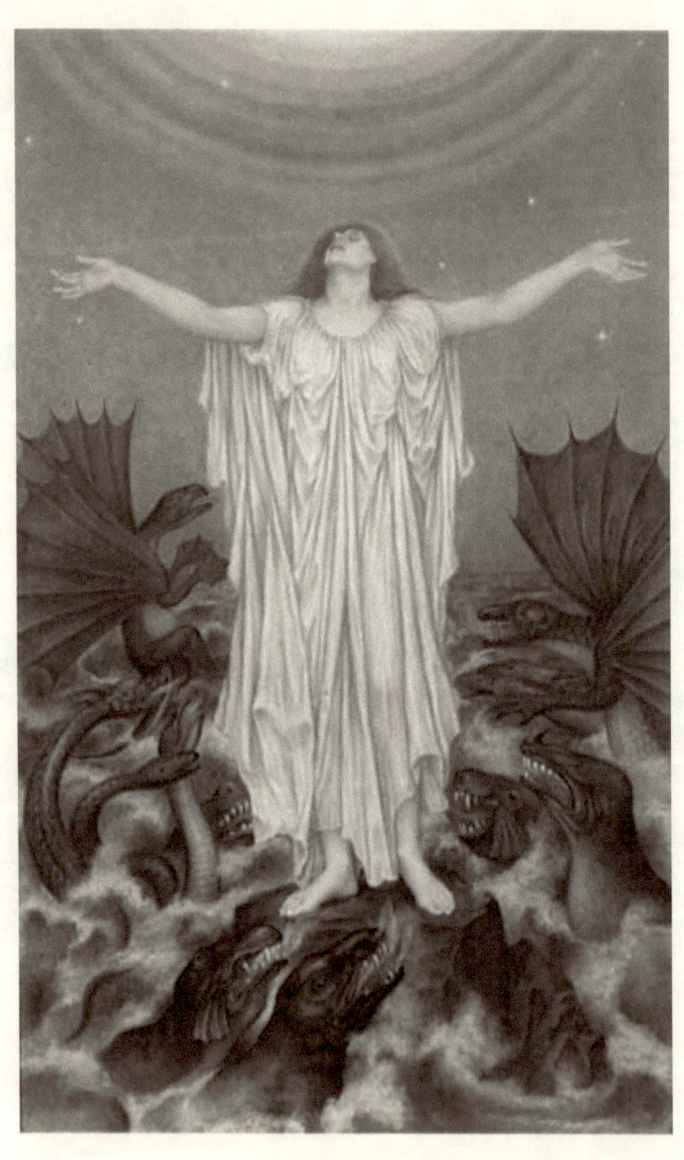

S.O.S.
Oil on canvas

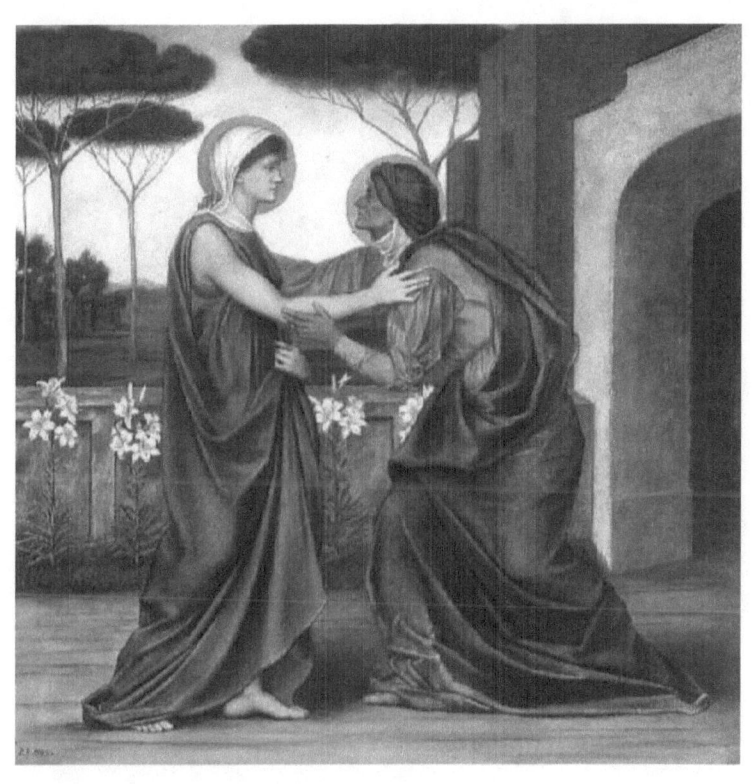

The Visitation (1883)
Oil on canvas

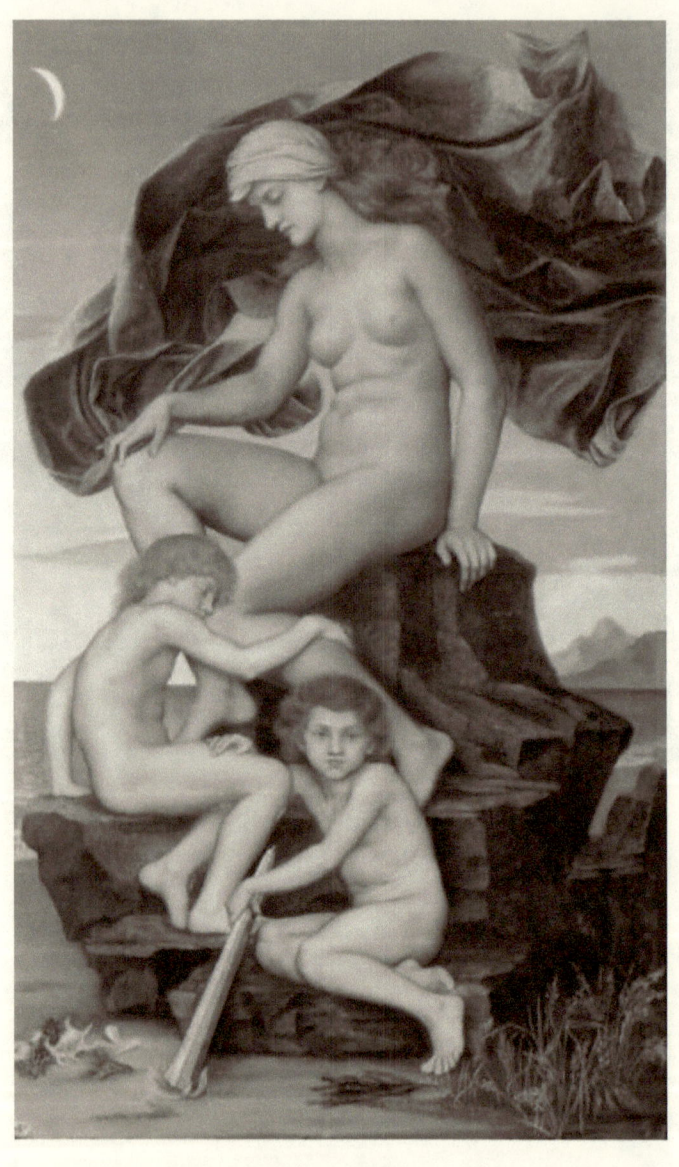

Sleep and Death, the Children of the Night (1883)
Oil on canvas

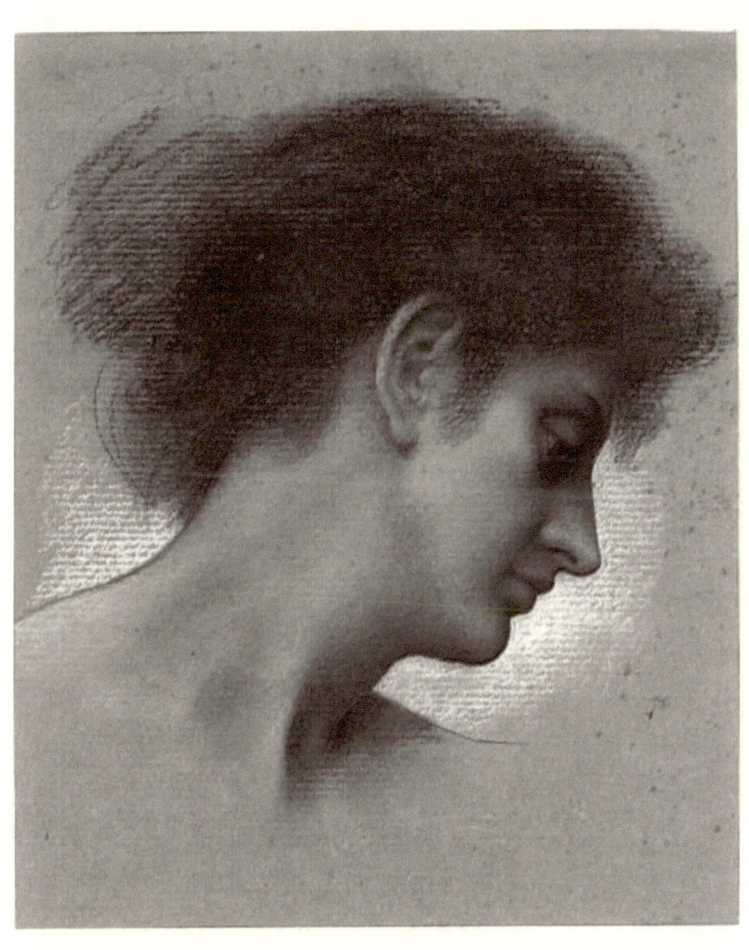

Study of a Head I
Pastel

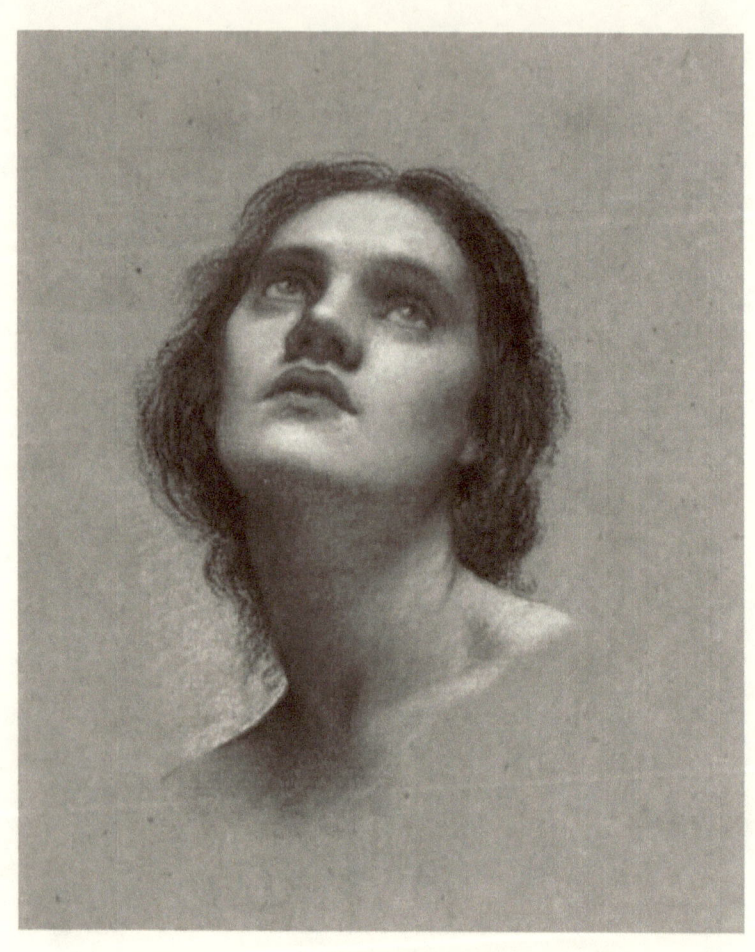

Study of a Head II
Pastel

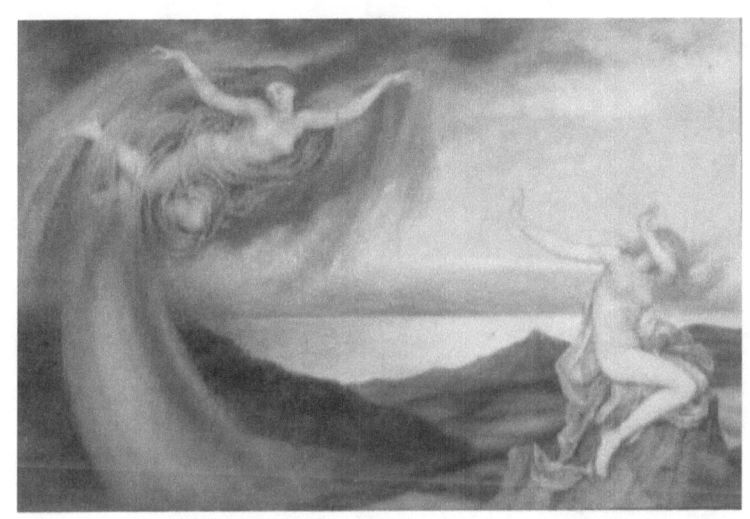

Sunbeam and Summer Shower
Oil on canvas

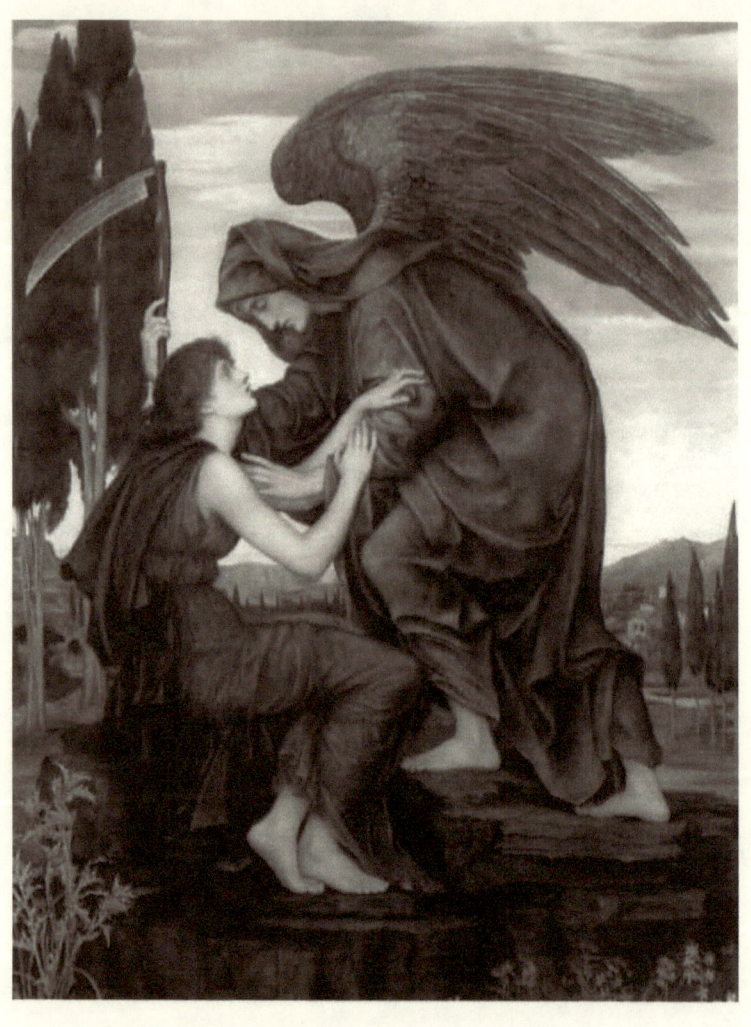

The Angel of Death (1890)
Oil on canvas

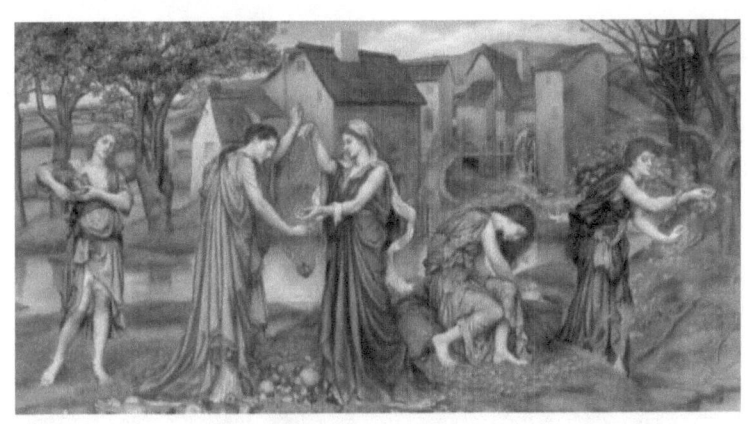

The Cadence of Autumn (1905)
Oil on canvas

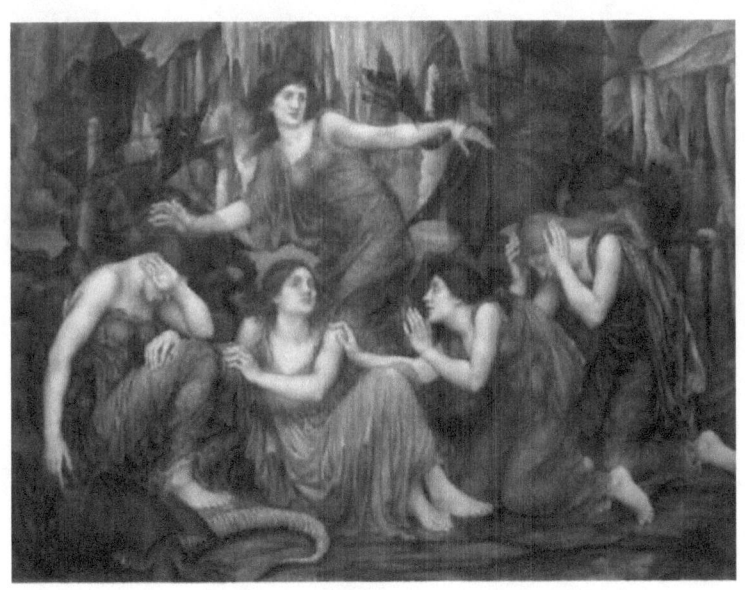

The Captives
Oil on canvas

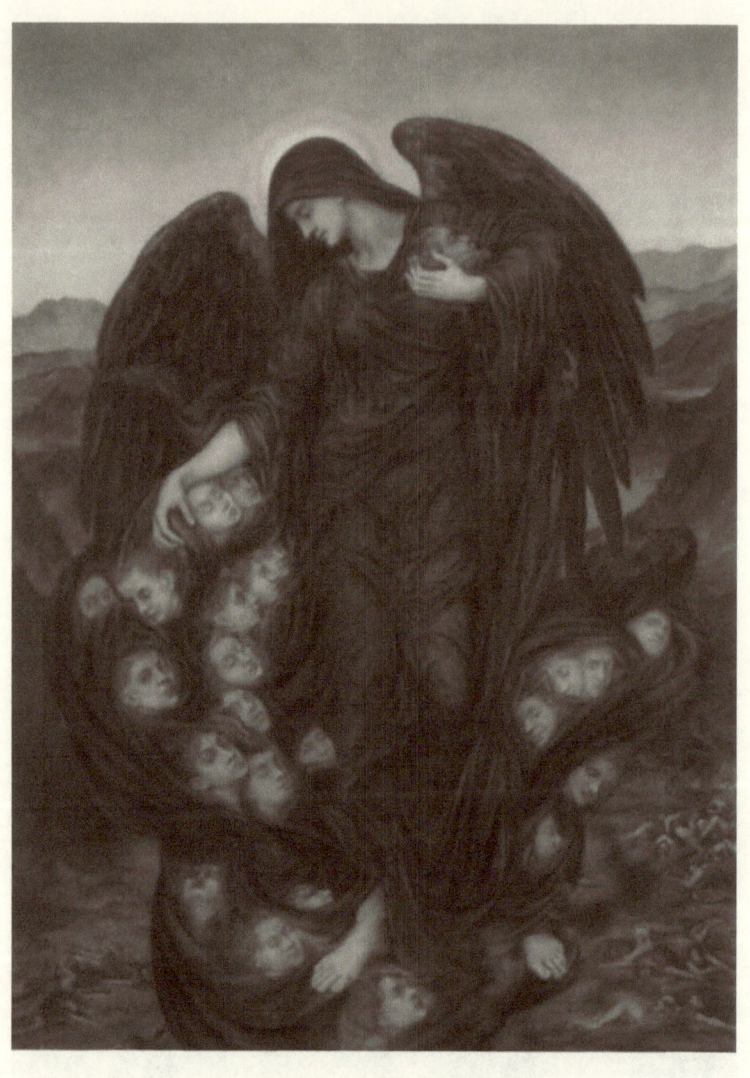

The Field of the Slain (1916)
Oil on canvas

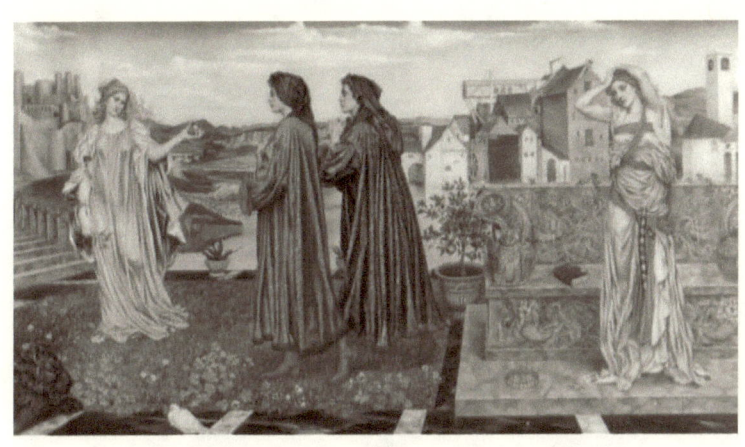

The Garden of Opportunity (1892)
Oil on canvas

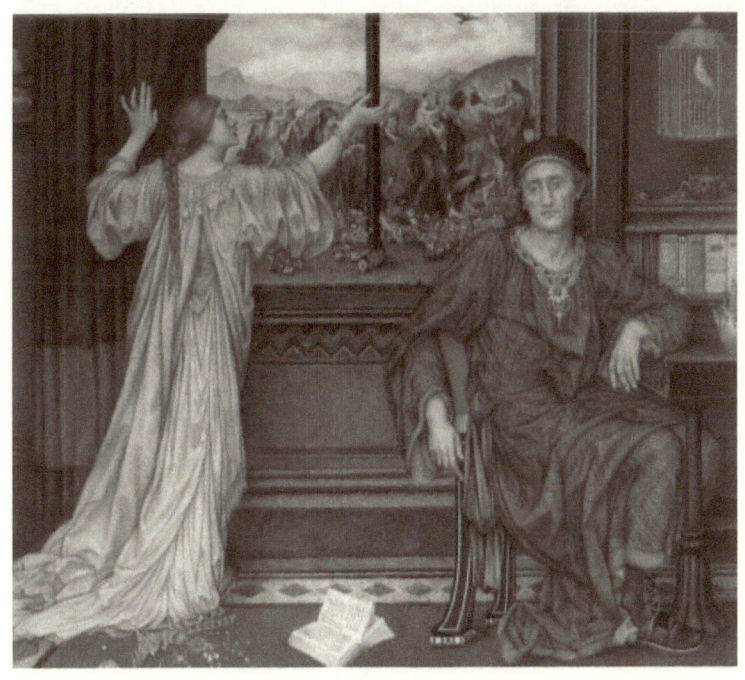

The Gilded Cage (1919)
Oil on canvas

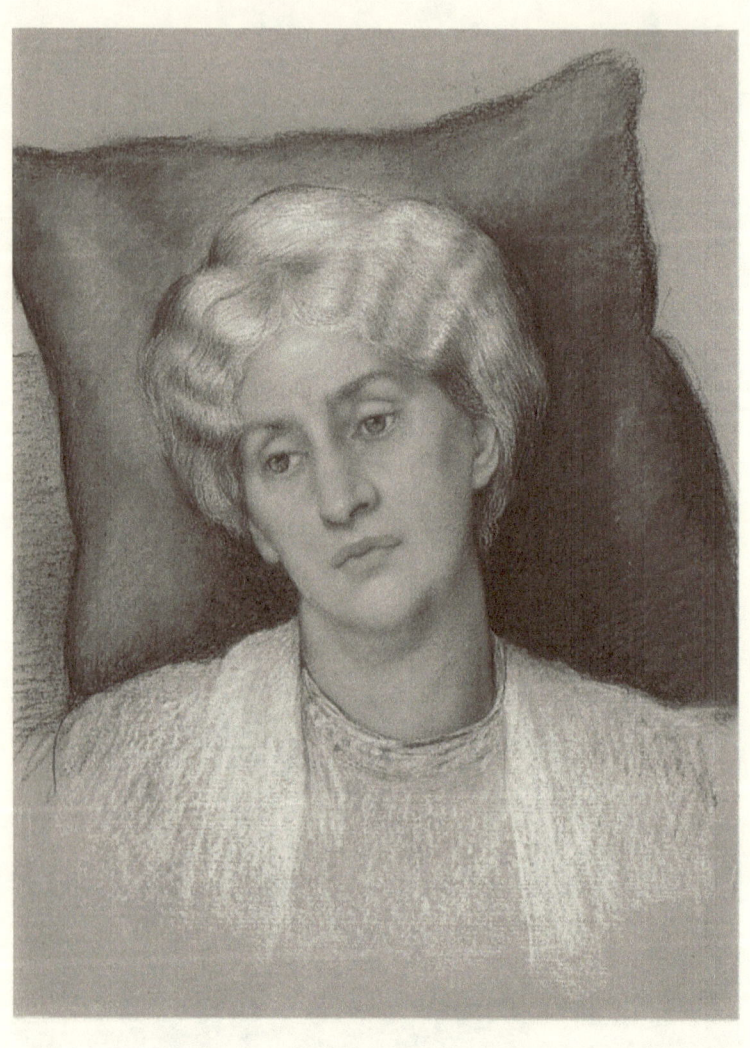

Portrait of Jane Morris (1904)
Pastel

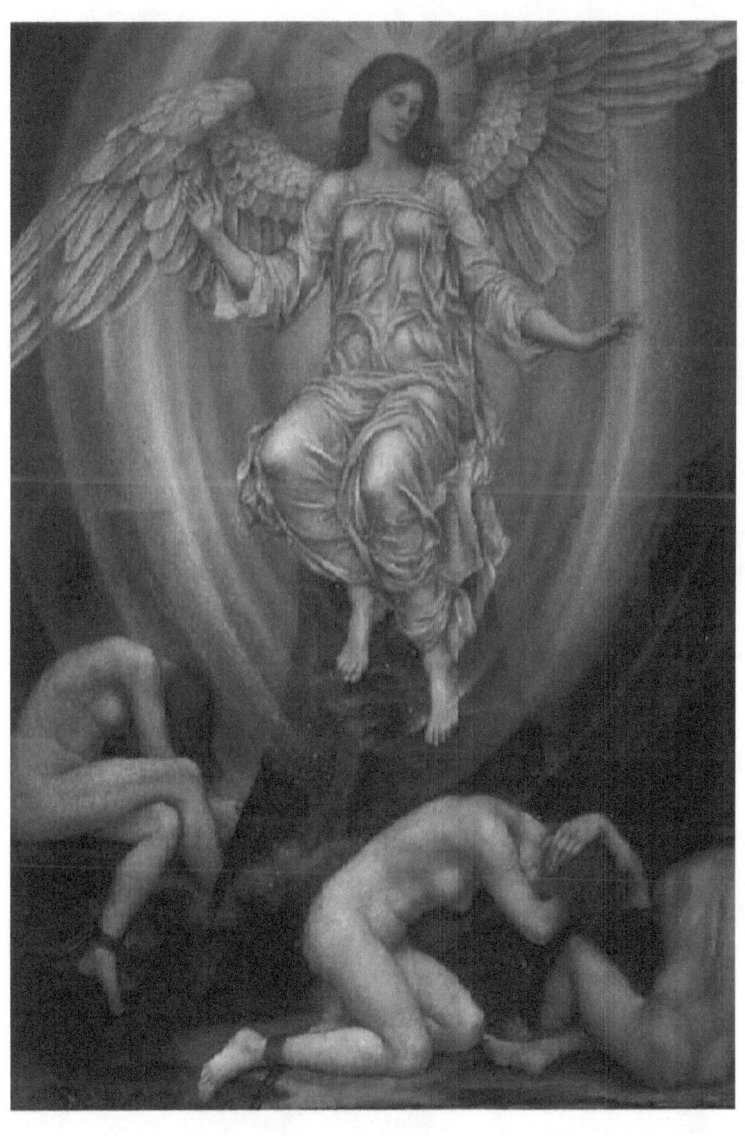

The Light Shineth in Darkness and the Darkness
Comprehendeth It Not
Oil on canvas

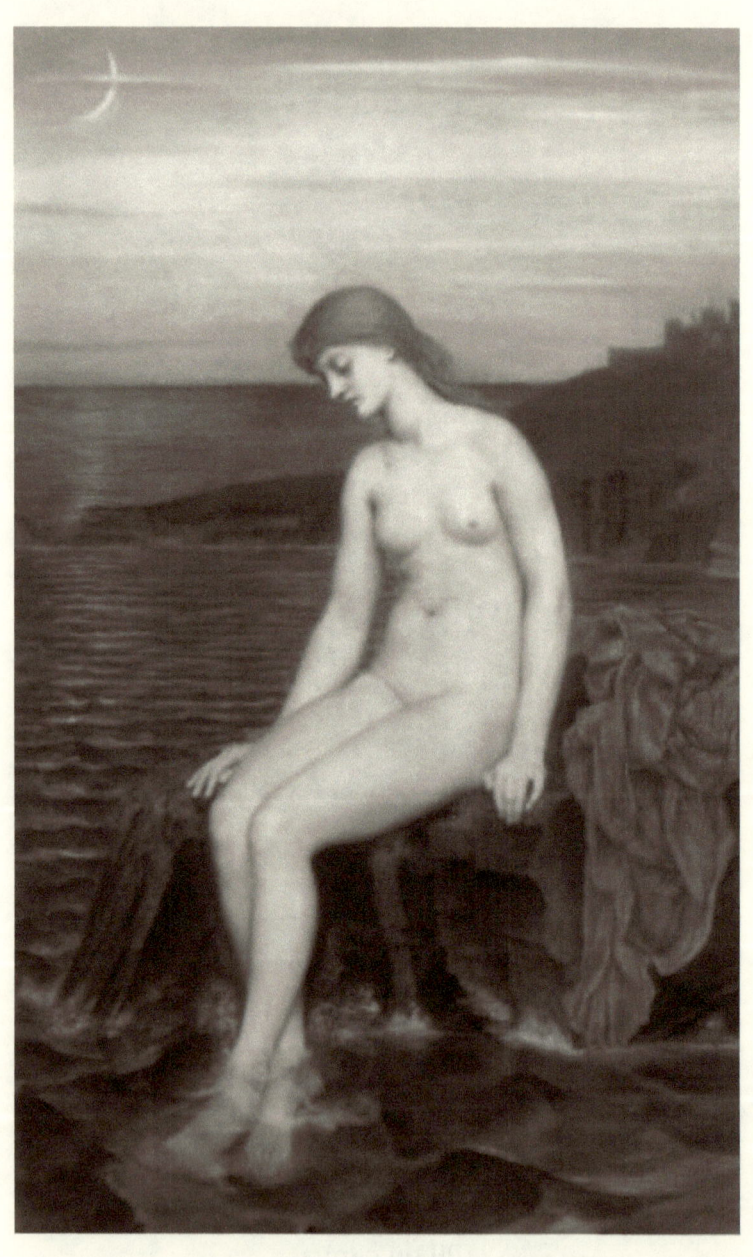

The Little Sea Maid (c. 1888)
Oil on canvas

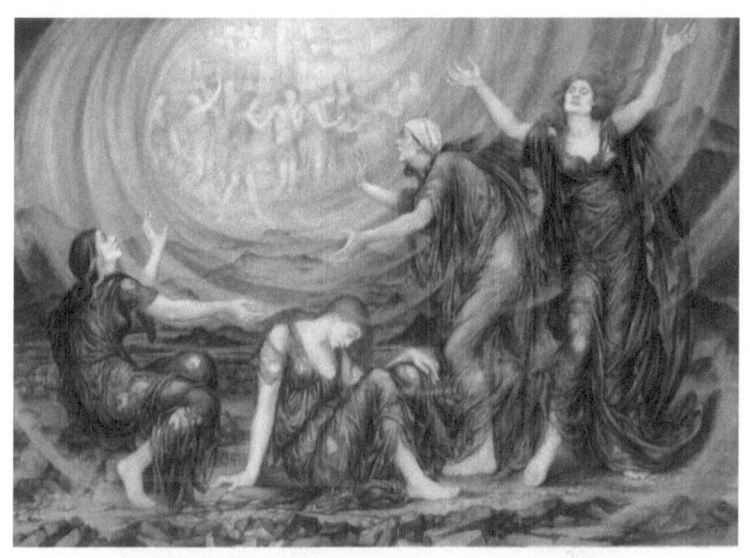

The Mourners
Oil on canvas

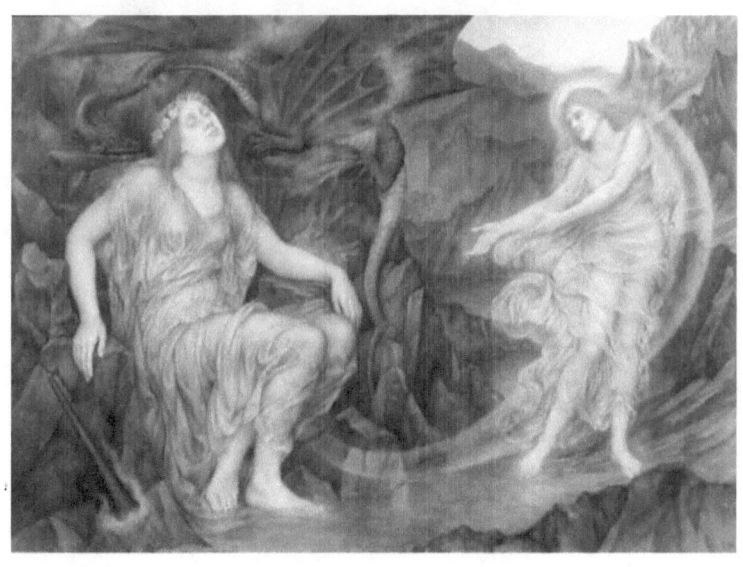

The Passing of the Soul
Oil on canvas

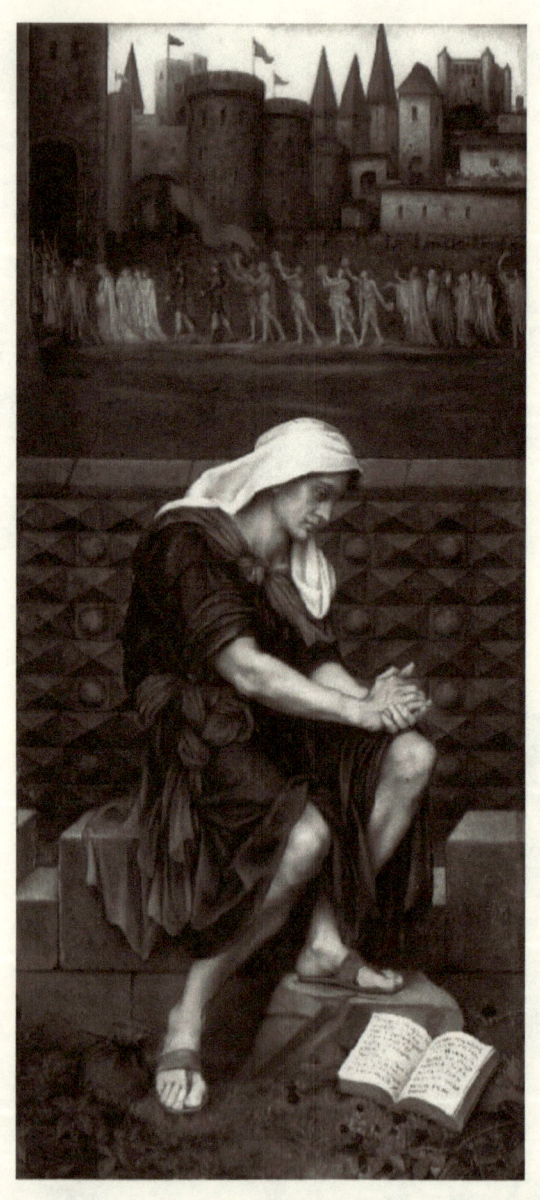

The Poor Man Who Saved the City (1901)
Oil on canvas

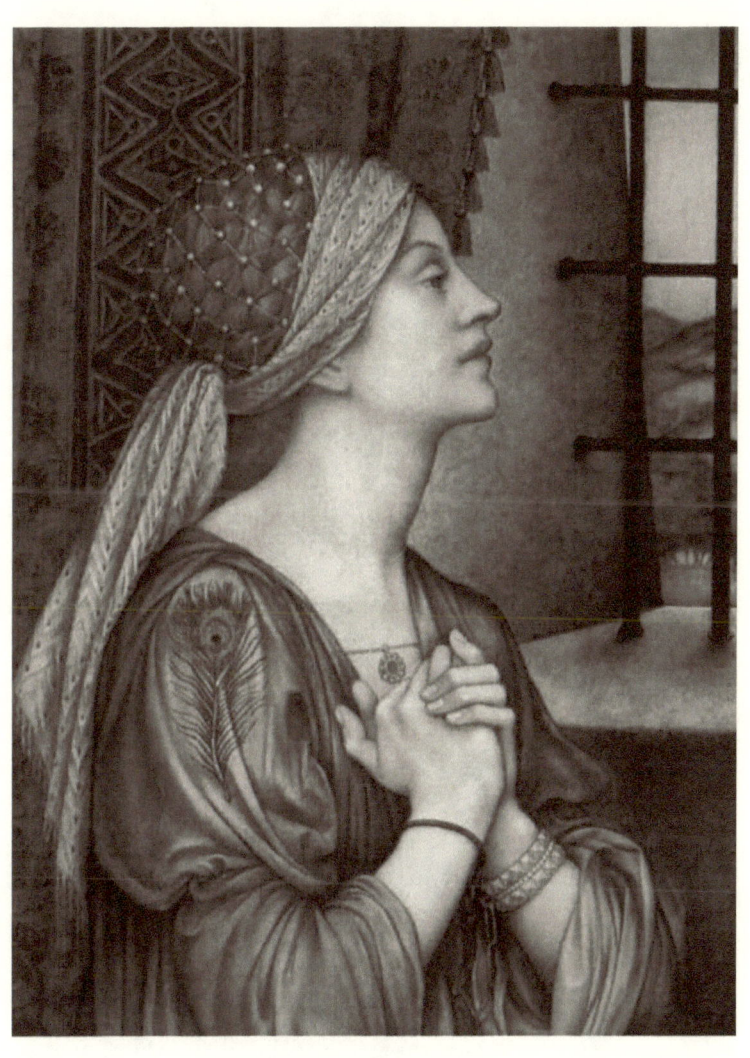

The Prisoner (1907)
Oil on canvas

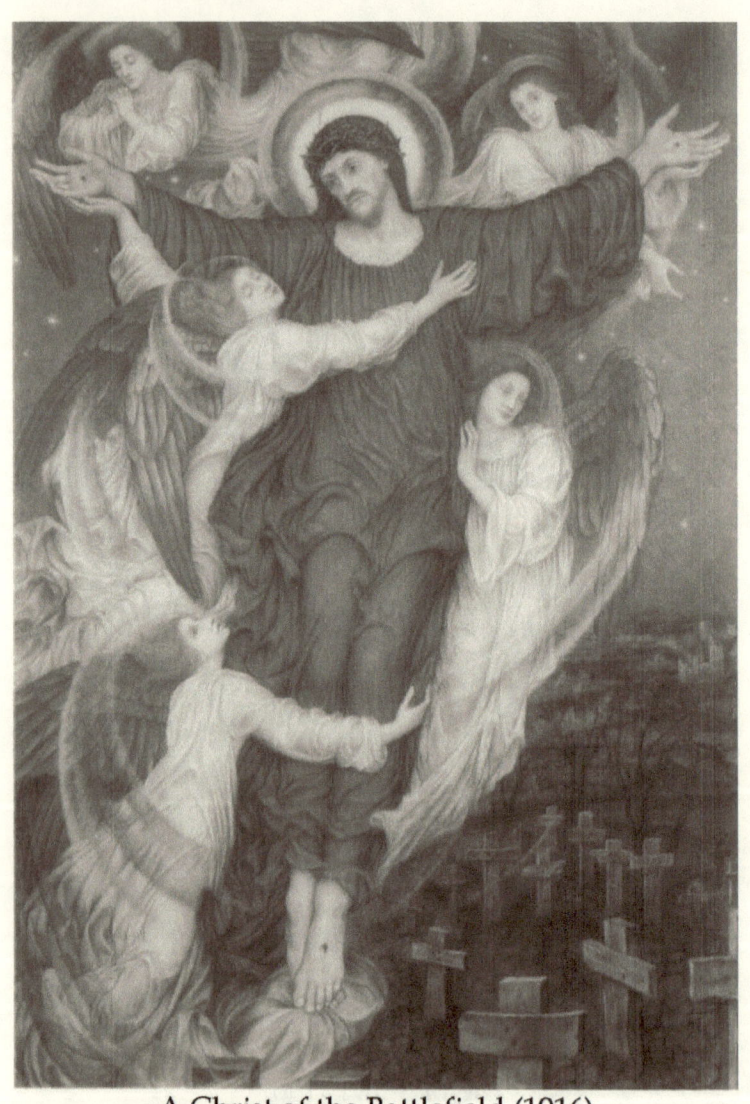

A Christ of the Battlefield (1916)
Oil on canvas

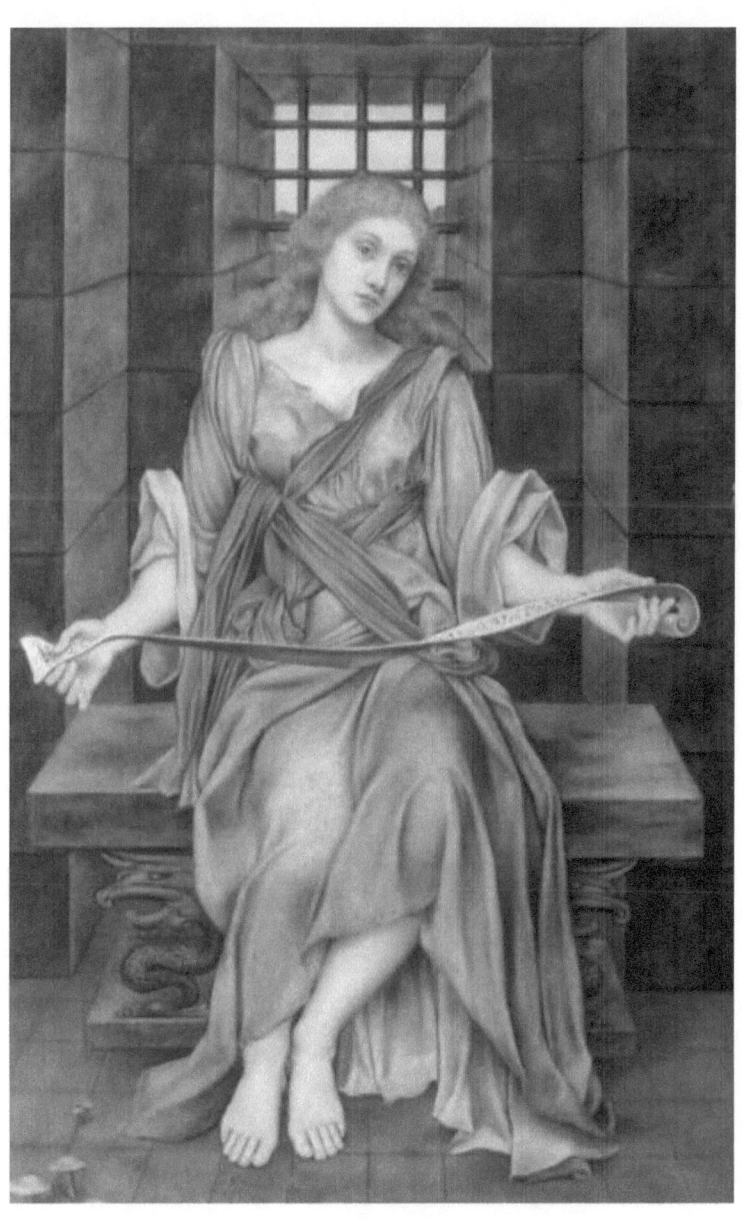

The Soul's Prison House (1888)
Oil on canvas

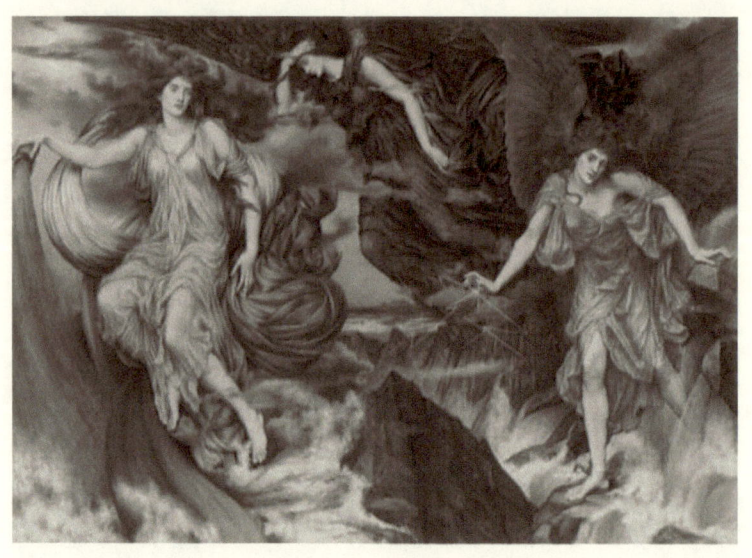

The Storm Spirits (1900)
Oil on canvas

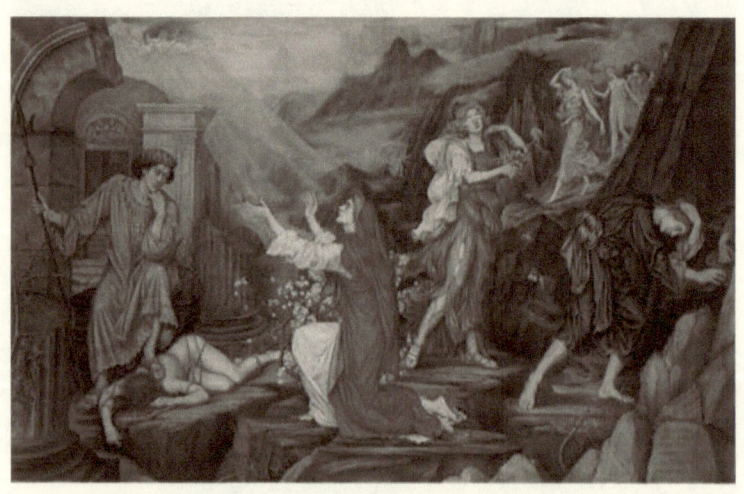

The Valley of the Shadows (1899)
Oil on canvas

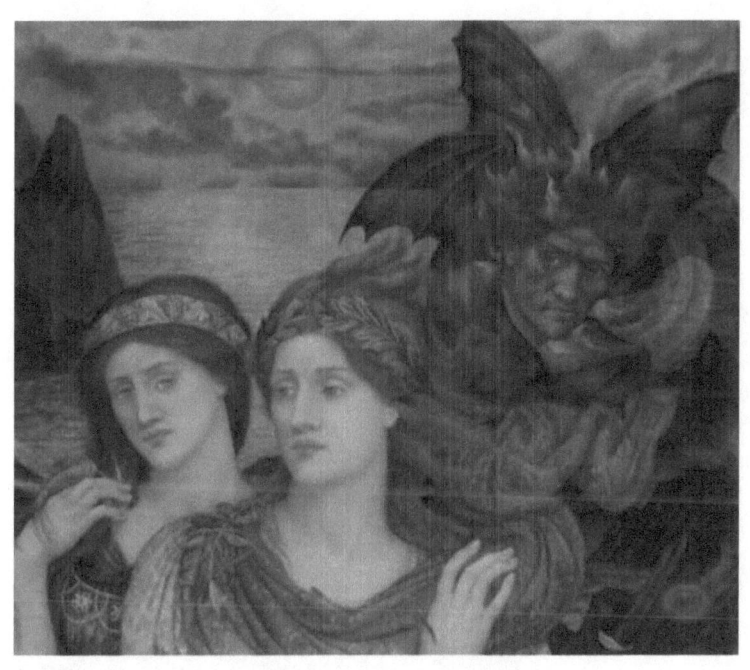

The Vision (c. 1914)
Oil on canvas

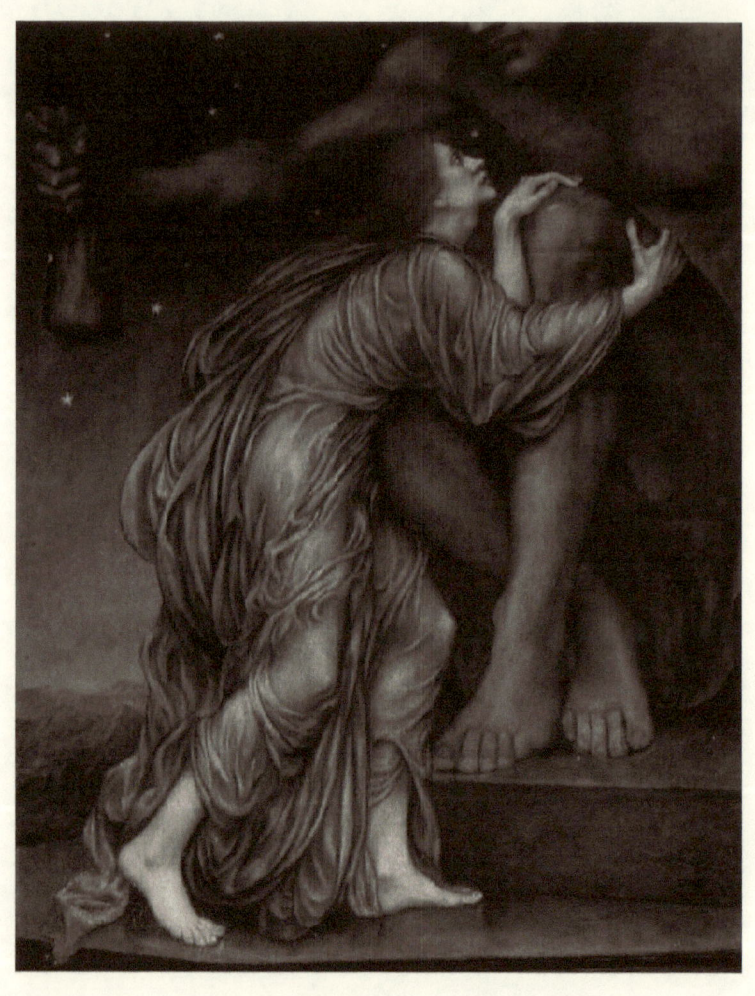

The Worship of Mammon (1909)
Oil on canvas